365 Ways through 365 Days

Earl Jackson

Printed in the United States of America

First Printing, April 2015

ISBN-10: 099604034X

ISBN-13: 978-0-9960403-4-1

Missing Button Publications

Publisher: Missing Button Publications

Cover Design: Heidi Peralta

Introduction

Hello, my name is Earl Jackson, and I am the author of this book. I wrote this particular book because I felt that people in general lacked the needed motivation, inspiration, and encouragement to get through their daily struggles. While this book is sectioned into weeks, it is intended to be a daily reader and contains quotes* and explanations to help you get through whatever it is you are going through. With this book, I hope to changes lives, to inspire the uninspired, and to motivate the unmotivated. We, as human beings, all go through tough times, and we don't always know how to cope with what we are going through. With this book, I want to provide an alternative option to help someone else get through their struggles in a positive and uplifting way, hopefully preventing the development of bad habits and an unhealthy lifestyle.

--Earl

*Some quotes included are original, and others paraphrase or have been inspired by well-known/famous quotes.

A note from the Editor:

This was an amazing project for me to collaborate with Earl on. I worked with Earl on his first book, *A Spirit of Perseverance*, and his story blew me to pieces. His storytelling had a way of captivating me and kept me turning page after page. As expected, this book was no different. While the subject matter is vastly different, Earl still has a way of tapping into your soul and making you want better, of making you want to be a better version of yourself. He gives you that extra push to go after your dreams and to reach for the unknown. It was reading this book that confirmed that I was indeed on the right path as an editor, and that I was pursuing *my* dream. I highly recommend sharing this book with anyone you think could use the motivation to get moving, or even those who just want confirmation that they are heading in the right direction. Don't ever be afraid to reach for your dreams!

--Britny

Pursuing the Positive

Week 1:

☐1. **"Keep waiting for the right moment, and you will wait forever."**

There will almost never be a perfect moment to do anything; something will always come up: life, death, bills, work, or school. There will always be something in life that hinders you in some way. In order to be successful, stop trying to plan every *exact* moment of your life because you won't win that battle. The best thing you can do is react and adapt to the things that happen in life that are out of your control. Go be great!

☐2. **"In life we are not promised happiness, but we are allowed to pursue happiness. It is up to us to decide what we are willing to endure in that pursuit of happiness."**

If you aren't happy with your life, it's your own fault. The first step in acknowledging that is taking responsibility. Take a minute to look at the events that have led up to your unhappiness. Were they all bad decisions? Did you have the right intention with every decision you made? The good thing is from this day forward you have the power to do whatever makes you happy. However, whether or not you are willing to embrace the hard times that come with making your life better is completely in your hands. No one else can take care of the hard work for you. Nobody can create happiness for someone else; you can only create that for yourself.

☐3. **"Do what you love so when situations become insane and overwhelming, your love for what you are doing keeps you going."**

A lot of people hate what they do for a living. Going to work every day, dreading what you do carries over into your personal life, and as a result, it can create unhealthy relationships, lifestyles, and it can even affect your health. People love to say, "If you hate your job, quit!" Well, it's not always that simple. You can't just quit on the spot because that affects your flow of income to provide for your most basic needs: food and shelter. What you can do, however, is work towards finding a better job. On the other hand, if you are already doing what you love, it can make life a lot easier. When overwhelming situations come up at work, it will be okay because you love what you do so much that you actually *embrace* the challenge instead of shy away from it. You will also have the mental focus to keep working hard, and to keep work separate from your personal life.

☐4. **"Create your foundation after you have established the blueprint. Be strict on yourself to stick with it, and in due time, you will see the signs of success."**

We all have dreams and sometimes we don't really know how to actually get started, or even where to begin. The only person who has a clear vision of your plan is *you*. Take some time to create your blueprint exactly how you want it. It will help you with whatever it is you are pursuing and it will allow you to stick with it. Remember, just because you fail a couple of times doesn't make *you* a failure.

☐5. **"Sometimes, you may find that you are stuck in the water and it's neck high. Do not panic! As long as your head is still above water, you will always have a chance."**

We all get overwhelmed by the things that happen in our lives, but that's okay! You *have* to continue to push through.

Life hits everybody, regardless of whether they are rich, famous, or poor. We all have different troubles we face; however, if you are still breathing, that means you still have a chance to overcome your current and future obstacles. Don't give up! Be strong!

☐6. **"The job you have right now, someone else would die for that opportunity. Stop looking at it as an obligation and look at it more like an opportunity."**

Yes, some jobs aren't the best—but before you complain— think about the people who don't have a job. I'm sure you know one or two people who would *love* to have your job. Be grateful for what you have! Once you take something for granted, you no longer cherish it.

☐7. **"If you don't have a reason to justify what you do, you will never take it seriously."**

If what you are chasing after has no value or no purpose, you will only be willing to go through so much adversity. You need to find a reason for why you do what you do, so that when you get to that point of wanting to turn around or quit, your reason keeps you motivated to push through.

Grinding. We're not giving up this week!

Week 2:

☐8. **"Remember that really talented person who gave up? Neither do I, and I'm pretty sure no one else does either. Keep pushing!"**

Giving up should *not* be an option. You will hear the word "no" plenty of times, but take the word "no" simply as an opportunity to try again. You can't keep giving up when things get a little tough. Remember, tough times don't last, but tough people do.

☐9. **"Working on your craft builds confidence, and confidence pushes you to make it a routine. Repetition creates skills, and skills bring you a job."**

In whatever dreams or goals you are trying to accomplish, you have to continuously work on them. Make them a habit, and by doing that, you'll build self-confidence, even when people tell you that you can't do whatever it is you have your mind set on achieving. Keep that work ethic, and watch your dreams become a reality.

☐10. **"The reason you keep giving up and giving in is because you keep looking at how far you have to go. Instead, look at how far you have come."**

A wise man once said, "A journey of a thousand miles begins with one step." If you keep looking at how far you have to go, it will be even harder for you to start your journey. Try taking it step by step, as if you were trying to build a wall. If you were to build a wall, you physically cannot lay ten bricks at a time. You only can lay *one* brick at a time; each brick needs the brick before it to be laid as perfectly as possible in order for any progress to be made. Eventually, you will have built a sturdy wall. Go build your wall!

☐**11. "Never start anything expecting not to finish, that's quitting before you began."**

I don't believe in having a Plan B; if you plan for a Plan B that means you never intended for Plan A to work in the first place. If you spend time creating a Plan B, C, and so on, you can't put all the necessary energy and effort into making sure Plan A works. Focus on Plan A and do what it takes to get it done.

☐**12. "Don't make decisions based on what people think of you; they don't have the right or the privilege of putting you in Heaven or Hell. Only God can do that. You have to be able to neglect the negativity."**

People will doubt you, discourage you, and disapprove of you. You can't let what they think of you blur your vision and hinder the choices that you make when it comes to *your* life. Remember, the decisions you make for yourself are ones that you have to live with; nobody else will bear the fruit or the burden of those choices.

☐**13. "It's as simple as this, how bad do you want it? If you kind of want it, you will kind of work for it. If you *really* want it, you will work continuously for it, even when nobody is watching."**

Everyone says they want to get to the next level, but the question is, do you have that next level work ethic? It isn't all about the work ethic, but you have to maintain the ability to be consistent at working hard all of the time. Working when nobody is watching is key because when the lights come on, that will be your opportunity to take people by surprise.

☐14. **"The difference between successful people and unsuccessful people is when they hear the word 'no'. To successful people, 'no' means, 'Try again'. To unsuccessful people, that same word means, 'I can't do it'. Be willing to try over and over again until you get it right."**

"No" can be a hard word to digest; nobody likes to hear it. If you keep pushing, you will get what you are working towards. Take the word "no" and think of it as, "Not yet". The time you accept the word "no" and use it as an excuse not to try is when you have decided to give up on yourself.

Perspective and Production

Week 3:

☐ **15. "Eliminate those bad investments, such as bad habits and bad relationships; they take up too much time that you could be using productively elsewhere."**

Get rid of the bad apples in your basket; they will spoil the whole bunch. Cut the negative talk out, and cut the purposeless spending out. Stop wasting your time with—and on—individuals who don't want better for themselves, or you for that matter. Those people are lackadaisical, and their unenthusiastic persona can rub off on you, and trust me, you will find yourself going nowhere fast.

☐ **16. "Today is what you have. Tomorrow may never come, but if it does, it has its own worries."**

You may be going through a hard time and you may not know where your help is going to come from. Bills may be due next week, or maybe you don't know where you will get food from for tomorrow. Today, I want to tell you to just worry about tackling today's concerns. Focus on the next 24 hours. Tell yourself, "I will conquer today."

☐ **17. "Get up, and stop relying on that snooze button; it will only make you late."**

Eric Thomas said, "I don't need an alarm clock; my passion wakes me up." If you rely on that snooze button, plan on being late to wherever it is you needed to be. With each step needed to reach your ultimate goal, you have a certain time period where things have to be done, and if you keep putting them on hold—or "snooze"—you won't accomplish your ultimate goal, or you will just end up delaying the entire process. Go to sleep without your alarm clock and see how badly you really want it.

☐18. "You have to constantly keep in mind the big picture, sacrifice who you are now for who you want to become in the future."

Throughout your journey to get to your destination, you will have to give up the things that take up too much of your time and take time away from your dreams and your goals. Some of the things you may need to sacrifice are relationships, hanging out, social media, and/or spending. By making a sacrifice, something good will come from doing so, and you will advance to that next level. You will also gain more wisdom and knowledge when you sacrifice.

☐19. "You will fail, you will cry, you will lose people, you will lose money, and you may even be homeless. You may face all of those obstacles in pursuit of your dream. But think of it like this, people will *still* go through those things when they *do* have a job, and that's even worse. You might as well chase what you love and endure the struggle. Embrace the grind, and conquer defeat."

Failure is unshakable, crying is assured in life, and losing friends and family members is guaranteed. You will be placed in tight situations that cause money problems to occur. But if you have to go through all of that anyway, go through all of that for something you *want* to do, not a job, career, or lifestyle you aren't even passionate about. You can conquer anything you face; you just have to first believe that you can do it.

☐ **20. "You can do anything in the world, including not doing anything at all."**

Anything in the world you want to accomplish, you can. The only thing you can't accomplish is something you chose not to accomplish because you gave up. Stop giving up so easily!

☐ **21. "Life is about change, and if you decide not to adjust to your circumstances accordingly, you will be a part of the 'lost and the left out'."**

The good thing about change is you can decide what you want to change. Your changes may include relationships, jobs, eating habits, and your belief system. See, the thing about the world is that it changes every day, whether you decide to adapt or not, events happen, people grow, and new things are invented. Get moving, or get left!

Going through it and Getting through it

Week 4:

☐ **22. "Give it all you got, overwork exhaustion, create a new normal, and speak success into your vision."**

In anything you do, give it your all, not just your best. If you only dish out your best, my thinking is you still have *something* left to give. To me, giving your all means you leave nothing left in the tank. Many successful people gave their all at some point throughout their careers, and that's why they are where they are in life today. Create a new you who gives your all in everything you do, continuously speak success into your plan, and watch as the signs begin to appear.

☐ **23. "If you want to give up on others, that's your choice. But don't ever give up on you."**

Sometimes, you just have to give up on others because it's the right thing to do for *you*. You give up on people through your actions, your words, and even with your thoughts. Just make sure that you don't do anything, say anything, or think anything that shows—or even hints—that you are giving up on yourself. Even though it isn't always our intention, when we give up on people, we do so with the desire to remove the dead weight, so that we can move on with our lives and get closer to our goals.

☐ **24. "What you are going through is not meant to destroy you, it's meant to develop you."**

Right now, it may feel like what you are going through is tearing you apart, and you begin to think that you just can't take it anymore. Don't think that way! Look at it as though you are lifting weights. When you lift weights, what you are really doing is stretching your muscles to tear the old space apart to create room for new muscle mass. The rest period *after* lifting weights is when you actually build more strength. So, while you think your struggles are tearing you apart, they are actually making you much stronger than you could ever imagine.

☐25. "On the way up you will drop some dead weight; they can only pretend to like you for so long."

When you are moving forward, there will be people who want to be around you just for the ride. You will recognize by their actions that the love isn't genuine. Then there are some people who have been around for while, but you have outgrown them and they start to stunt your growth. I'm not saying that you should cut people off, simply put them in perspective with what you are trying to do for you.

☐26. "You possess talents and gifts that you have yet to discover."

The only way to find out what those gifts are is by getting out of your comfort zone; you have to stretch and bend yourself in order to adapt to whatever comes your way. You have to see how much discomfort you can endure. It will be hard and uncomfortable, but it's worth it. At that next level, there is nothing but great things waiting for you. Embrace it when it comes.

☐27. "Develop confidence, with that mentality you can win even before the grind starts."

Never go into anything expecting the outcome to be nothing less than success or victory. A majority of successful people have the mindset that failure is not an option, so they go into every problem or situation knowing that it will be solved, or that it will be handled. The key to being successful is understanding that how you think mentally affects what you do physically.

☐28. "If strangers support you before your so-called 'friends', it's time to do some reevaluating."

This type of behavior, or anything like it, is a sign of jealousy. You need to analyze each and every relationship you have with the people around you, and determine who is really there to support you and who is only there to tear you down. The people you barely know are the ones who tend to support you the most, and if that's the case, you have some things to reconsider.

Let's not make things difficult

Week 5:

☐ **29. "Know that perfection is not securable, but in striving for perfection, greatness is attainable."**

Perfectionists never reach perfection, but among the most critical perfectionist, greatness has been achieved. One of the biggest false sayings is, "Practice makes perfect." That is wrong; you can practice the incorrect way and perfect the wrong thing. The correct saying is, "Practice makes permanent." With that being said, practice, practice, practice, but do it the *correct* way to make it permanent, and you never know, greatness could be just around the corner.

☐ **30. "Passion and desire can't blend if you are lackadaisical."**

Being lazy when you want to be successful is like being on a diet but only eating sweets, bread, and candy. It will never work; it makes no sense at all because you are doing everything you *aren't* supposed to be doing. Stop wanting the shine before the grind! Don't be discouraged by the process, it's never pretty, but it's definitely worth it in the end. Remember, a beautiful butterfly was once a slimy caterpillar.

☐ **31. "Are you hungry or starving for success?"**

You really can't answer this question from your mouth; your work ethic has to do the "talking". Hungry is doing what everyone else would do, putting in a couple of extra hours here and there. Meanwhile, starving is putting in the work every little chance you have an opportunity to do so. A lot of people are hungry, so to be comfortable they will work two jobs. The people who are starving, they may work two or three jobs *and* be enrolled in school. Get an attitude of starvation; this world is full of give and take. But not enough people are willing to give what it takes.

☐ **32. "When you can sit down, sit instead of standing, but if you can lay down, lay down instead of sitting."**

You have to learn to stop making things hard for yourself; sometimes, you create your own trials and tribulations. You have to start thinking things all the way through. Weigh the positives and negatives, and know that you have to live with whatever you choose. Every problem isn't rocket science.

☐ **33. "Opportunities may come once in a lifetime, make a lifetime of that opportunity."**

Opportunities will present themselves, but you'll never know how many you will get. So, if—and when—the knock comes, you have to take full advantage. You have to be *all* in, or let someone else have that opportunity because they will take it much more seriously than you will. Trust and believe someone else is waiting for that opportunity that you might have taken for granted.

☐ **34. "If you are not doing what you love, why are you doing it?"**

Love and happiness coexist, so if what you are doing doesn't bring you joy and happiness, why do you do it? I hope it isn't because of the benefits, such as money, status, or material things, because all of that is only temporary excitement. Eventually, those things will become old, and unhappiness can set in once again.

☐35. "Today is the day you decide to take a chance on you."

You are always saying, "I will start something..." and ending it with the next week, the next month, or the next year. Well, today is the day you start! Stop pushing your dreams back for no reason. Your time is limited on this earth, and you don't know when your time is up.

Get serious and make things happen

Week 6:

☐36. "Take your life seriously. Don't let people waste your time because time isn't promised."

Your life is filled with so many endless possibilities, and you have so many gifts and abilities you have yet to even experience. Until you get away from the normal and push past the uncomfortable, you will stay where you are in life. You will never find out what you could have done, or who you could have been if you never challenged yourself.

☐37. "If you want to drop the dead weight, whether it's the people around you, or even yourself, start off with dropping the excuses and the weight will follow. Don't make an excuse to keep unwanted people or unwanted weight in your life."

We tend to make excuses for why we can't make changes in our life. The sad thing is we make ourselves actually *believe* it. You have to start holding yourself accountable for your actions. Excuses make you late, and being late gets you left behind.

☐38. "Don't let greed poison your soul and turn you from good principles. How you treat people plays a big part in how successful you can become."

In this day and age, everybody wants to be rich; that's fine and dandy, but could you handle the pressure if you actually did become wealthy? If you were to accomplish whatever it is you set out to accomplish, will success change you as a person? Will you remain humble? The way you treat people can determine how far you go in life. Nobody wants to be around a conceited, stuck up individual. The change you want in your life requires you to adjust to your circumstances, while remaining the same person you were before you accomplished all of your goals because as easy as you got it, it can be gone even faster.

☐ 39. "You think too much and feel too little."

With some of your decisions, you tend to overthink a simple question when all you have to do is use your natural human instinct, your feelings. Don't try to use your head for a heart-seeking answer; you may regret that in the long run.

☐ 40. "Stop letting your knowledge fool you into thinking you know everything. Shut up and listen sometime."

You may not always be wrong, but for certain, you are not always right. You want answers to the problems, but you aren't willing to shut up and let someone else talk or respond to the situation. Someone who isn't as closely attached to the situation as you are may have a better outlook and be able to see more clearly.

☐ 41. "Wake up today and make a difference in someone else's life, and see how much better you feel."

It is so easy for us to wake up and start our day making sure that we have everything we want and need. Today, challenge yourself to make someone else smile. Go buy someone a meal, cut someone's grass, or go make someone else excited to be alive.

☐42. **"Risk more than is required to get further than you thought you could go."**

Some of us are always skeptical about trying new things because we fear the outcome. In order to be successful, you have to be willing to take risks, whether it is financially, making big decisions, or putting relationships on hold to keep yourself from getting distracted.

Attitude determines altitude

Week 7:

☐43. **"Dismiss mediocrity, release contentment, and strive for greatness to exceed expectations."**

Words like, "normal", "average", "satisfied", "pleased", and "at ease" are all traps to stay where you are in life. Nobody wants to stay at the same job without a raise, nobody wants to live in the same apartment forever, nobody wants to drive the same car forever, and nobody wants to wear the same set of clothes for the rest of their lives. In order to change those things, you have to change the way you work, the way you think, and the way you act. Do so with the intent to better yourself, and to put yourself in a better position.

☐44. **"You should not measure your success based on how much money you make or what you own. Instead, your success should be measured based on the lives you have impacted in a positive manner. The memories you give a person last much longer than anything you can buy them."**

Your personal status is irrelevant. If you can't motivate, uplift, and inspire the youth—and many others—to follow your blueprint, allowing them to experience some of the same success you did, you are selfish, and once you leave this life, your life will have been meaningless. You left the world with nothing to learn from and with nothing to gain from you. It's okay to gain all of your heart's desires, but don't ever think for one second that you are bigger than the next person. We are all placed on this earth to make it a better place in one way or another, so get to work!

☐45. **"Do not ignore discipline, trust it, for that is the only way to become successful."**

Discipline is something that is needed in order to get that body you want, for example. You can't eat the fried foods, the sweets, or drink the sodas. You have to *discipline* yourself to eat right and to work out. When it comes to the deadlines for writing your book, you must set time aside to devote to writing. Using that time for nothing else requires some discipline.

☐46. **"Live the life you preach. Don't let your lifestyle be the total opposite of what you speak."**

We all have great advice to give to others, but a lot of people give advice and don't use that same advice for themselves. Before you try to tell someone how, what, or when they should do something, make sure you have yourself in order. You have to make sure *your* shoes are on the right foot before you try to tell someone else how to tie *their* shoes.

☐47. **"Don't let someone else's pain be your pleasure.**

Just because things aren't going your way right now, don't feed off of someone else's downfall to make yourself feel better. We have to be able to pick others up in their time of need, even when we are going through tough things ourselves. Some people are mentally stronger than others, and as a result, you don't know how far on the edge the next person is. Your words of encouragement could save someone's life.

☐48. **"At some point in time, you need to realize that the people who started with you are the same ones who can't finish with you. Your race is your own."**

In life, we speak about loyalty, and people really have a messed up understanding of the word. Your loyalty is to yourself, first of all. You can be honest and respectful of everyone, but there is no way to be *loyal* to everyone. True friends tell each other how they feel, and they are honest. There's no way to be loyal to yourself *and* to someone else at the same time. If you don't agree with what they do or what they believe in, you are going against the loyalty you should have to yourself. Be loyal to yourself, and go confidently in the direction of your dreams. Your journey is your own and only you can reach your destination.

☐49. **"Stop allowing people to hold you down because that's what they will do when given the opportunity. Instead, ask for people to hold you accountable."**

This is a problem a lot of us have; we have too many people in our circle who bring no value. They talk negatively, and your goals and your dreams don't align with each other's in no way, shape, or form. Find people who hold you responsible for making excuses for the things you don't accomplish. Stay away from the people who tell you, "Don't worry about it, you will be okay!" That is stunting your growth, and you will never reach your potential if you are around people who do not challenge you to be better.

Turn that grind into shine!

Week 8:

☐50. **"The reason you won't become successful is because you keep making excuses for why you won't do something. Stop making excuses and make changes."**

It's so easy to say why you aren't doing something; the challenge is shutting up and getting the work done. The moment you decide to be quiet and just grind, watch as positive things begin to happen in your life.

☐51. **"Chase your dream with a one-way ticket."**

We all get a vision, which is another word for "dream". Now, the only way to reach it is to fully act on it. Don't go in with a Plan B because if you do, you are already planning to fail. You might fail, but keep working at it. Steve Jobs got fired from his own company, but eventually, he was rehired. You better stick with your dreams, or work for someone else who never gave up on theirs.

☐52. **"Perseverance is the mindset and the work ethic you have to work harder even after the hard work you already did. Don't complain about working hard when you know deep down inside you still have more to give."**

We all have a comfort zone and we all have different levels of discomfort we can take. The problem is we always get to our comfort zone and say that is enough for us. In doing so, we never grow. For instance, if you go to the weight room and you lift 100 pounds every time, that's your comfort zone. But if you go in and add 50 pounds more each time, it will be more difficult for you to feel comfortable, but in the long run, it will make you stronger. Get out of that comfort zone; you know you have more to give, so stop cheating yourself.

☐53. "You know that breath you just took? It was a gift. Don't waste any more of your gifts."

Remember, you were blessed to wake up today, that was a gift to you. Someone else was not blessed with that today. If you keep waking up, taking things and opportunities for granted, they, too, will be taken away from you. Don't waste your blessings or your gifts.

☐54. "One of the best feelings in the world is accomplishing something that people said you couldn't. The best part is knowing you're humble enough not to throw it in their faces. By not throwing it in their faces, that actually hurts them more than you mentioning it because you won't give them a reason to justify why they said you couldn't do it in the first place."

Everyone loves to prove someone wrong; it's human nature, but be humble about it. Honestly, what does bragging do for you? Make you prideful? Pride is an inwardly directed emotion, meaning it just makes you feel good and nobody benefits from that, not even you because no one likes to deal with prideful people. Just enjoy your accomplishments humbly. Trust me, that person already knows what you've accomplished, and they feel bad enough as it is for saying you couldn't do it.

☐55. "I'm going to keep it simple today, endurance. Whatever it is you are going through, endure the struggle. It will make you more humble when you get to wherever it is you are trying to go, and you will appreciate it that much more."

44

Every day presents a new challenge, whether it's just the rain, you ran out of toothpaste, or you woke up late for work. Those are all day changers if you let them affect you on top of the bigger problems that life throws at you. Death, sickness, homelessness, broken families, and abuse are some of the bigger things life throws at you. With that being said, conquer today and don't worry about tomorrow because tomorrow will bring a whole new set of challenges. Make the necessary adjustments to make today better however you can; it may not be easy, but getting through it is the key. When time passes, you will look back and smile for what you've been through and for the personal growth you see.

☐56. "As an athlete, your body will only be 100% the day *before* you ever started your sport. In life, there will be days you are sick, tired, or mentally out of it, and there will be other problems as well. Whatever the case might be, you won't be 100%, but you can't quit during the game, either. Finish strong!"

As an athlete, I have never been 100% after high school basketball. From college to professional basketball, I have had bruises, rolled ankles, and aches and pains from training, but I never quit because I love what I do. That's the same way you need to be in life; you may never have it all together at the same time, meaning there will always be a problem or situation to deal with, but you have to keep going. The world won't stop for your problems, so don't you stop for them, either. Love your life.

Realization, Fulfillment, and Fruition

Week 9:

☐ 57. **"You don't owe anyone an explanation for why you do what you do. Just make sure the decisions you make don't leave you questioning yourself. Go confidently in the direction of your dreams."**

You don't have to explain anything to anyone, just be careful; every action gets an equal or opposite reaction. Your life is your movie and you are the director. The choices you make determine if it's a blockbuster or a bust.

☐ 58. **"Just do it, stop thinking about it, whatever 'it' may be. ' Coulda, shoulda, woulda' are the last words of a regretful fool."**

Like Nike says, "Just Do It". If you keep contemplating on doing something, you leave room for doubt, and doubt is something that you cannot have influencing you. That will take you from being a dream chaser to daydreamer in the drop of a hat.

☐ 59. **"Drown yourself in positive possibilities. Be optimistic about every positive opportunity that comes about."**

Attract yourself to all things positive, from people, music, readings, news, to activities, and take advantage of the opportunities those encounters bring. The only time opportunities aren't available is when you decide not to open your mouth and create one.

☐ 60. "Even though it looks bad, it's still all good."

Your funds are low, your bills are backed up, you need new clothes, and your job is overwhelming, but guess what, you are still here. As long as that is the case, there is still hope out there. I'm sure you have been through a slump before and you have gotten through that—obviously—because you are reading this. What you are going through is just another testimony for you to share with someone else in order to help them get through their own storm. With that being said, it may look hopeless, but it's going to get better.

☐ 61. "Look at yourself in the mirror right now and say, 'I won't fail because if I do, others will suffer'."

Realize that your failure won't only hurt you. There are people who have invested in you. They've invested money and time, and there are other people who look up to you. They are *all* counting on you. Your success will change people's lives, and your failures will make people struggle. Live every day knowing that people are counting on you to give your best, and success is much bigger than your own personal gratification.

☐ 62. "You will never be good at whatever it is you do if there is no passion behind it."

Getting started is one of the hardest things to do, but what's harder is continuing to push even when you feel like giving up. There has to be a reason for why you do what you do. Your reason may be the loss of a loved one, proving wrong the people who doubted you, or maybe someone else is depending on you. But whatever that reason is, it will make it harder for you to quit because you are not doing it just for yourself.

☐63. **"Sometimes, the only time you will hear good things about yourself is when you tell yourself. You have to accept that."**

There are some people who just don't like to give credit to others. You have to be able to deal with that and push forward, anyway. Start looking in the mirror and give yourself compliments. It's important for you to be able to make yourself feel good before you allow others that privilege.

In pursuit of your purpose

Week 10:

☐64. **"The ability to be great is in each and every one of us, but the obedience and the work ethic is what we must dish out in order to achieve greatness. Today, be willing to do that."**

We all can achieve greatness, but the difference is that some of us get a whiff of tough wind and turn around, while the ones who become great endure the struggle. You have to welcome the struggle with open arms, knowing that success follows the struggle. You can't avoid struggle; the only way to get past it is to go through it. By going through it, you develop another level of tolerance. So, when that next struggle brings on a bigger challenge, your newly acquired tolerance level from your previous struggle has already elevated you towards future success.

☐65. **"You did not wake up on the wrong side of the bed, don't think that. Put your hand over your heart. You feel that? It's called purpose, find your reason."**

A lot of people have rough starts to the day, and as cliché as it may sound, people do say, "I woke up on the wrong side of the bed." Our thoughts determine our mindset and cause us to speak things into existence, and the things we speak aren't always positive. Waking up on the wrong side of the bed is allowing something so minor to have a huge impact on your life when it really should have no impact at all. Don't complain when things like that happen. Your time on earth is limited, so accomplish all you can before that day comes when you never wake up again.

☐ 66. "Don't spend your life trying to fit in; you were born to be different. Concentrate on being an anomaly."

We may share birthdays, clothes, and food, but we were all made uniquely with different talents and gifts. I don't believe anyone was blessed with a great gift of following, but that is something that was taught to us because we were taught to follow directions, laws, and plans. We were all blessed with our own minds and the ability to make decisions. Focus on what makes you happy, even if it is out of the norm.

☐ 67. "The only mistake you want to avoid is giving up; you can learn from everything else."

We all make mistakes, you are mistakenly wrong if you think that anyone is perfect. You can't be afraid to fail, or be afraid of making mistakes, because that is how you learn. You can't keep making the *same* mistake because then you clearly haven't learned anything. If that's the case, change the plan, not the goal.

☐ 68. "Today, look in the mirror and say, 'I'm better than pointing the finger at others for where I am in life. I am better than that'."

Face it, you are where you are in life because of the decisions and the choices you made. People might have influenced you, but you had the final say. With that being said, point the finger at yourself. Now that the blame is on you, get past it. It's time to move on. You now have today, and however else long you have left on this earth, to change your circumstances. Get to it!

☐ 69. "Today, I will ignore ignorance, neglect negativity, and disregard disrespect."

Ignorance, negativity, and disrespect are crabs in a barrel. Those things will bring you down so fast. You have to avoid people, jobs, events, and surroundings that have the potential to bring you down. They will halt your success and make you depressed. You are a positive person, so surround yourself with positivity. Speak it, live it, spread it, and watch it grow while you flourish.

☐ 70. "Bad things happen to test your character, remember that. Don't run away from the struggle, stick with it. Embrace it, defeat it, and conquer it."

Bad things do happen, but it's how you respond that determines what kind of person you are. Everyone will face some sort of adversity in their life, but how you deal with it dictates what kind of backbone you have. You can't run from every battle, and you can't win every one, either. In the end, what you go through will make you an even better person.

Welcoming the struggle

Week 11:

☐71. "You have a greater purpose than a hater's purpose. Stop worrying about them. You would never know you had any haters if you were solely focused on what you were trying to accomplish."

Everyone speaks about a hater, but no one truly knows who hates them. However, there are people who will hate on you just because you have a clear plan for your life and what you want to accomplish. All you can do is get over it. If you focus on you, and not who likes you, things would be a lot better for you. When someone makes the effort to hinder your progress, letting them see that they affect you gives them power, and they will keep trying to throw you off course. If you ignore it, they will eventually fade away and move on to something else. Either way, pay them no mind.

☐72. "You determine whether you win or lose in life, not your circumstances, not your surroundings, and not your past. You can change those circumstances and your surroundings, and you can move on from the past. Those are excuses, stop making them a habit."

It's easy to say that because a parent wasn't in your life you didn't have the proper guidance, or that because you grew up in a bad neighborhood that is the reason why you are where you are in life. We all are given a free choice; we can't choose who our parents are or how we grow up, but we *can* choose who we hang out with, what we watch, and whether we want to apply our time to developing our education or to having fun. The fact that you can identify your mistakes now eliminates the need for excuses, so stop trying to come up with new ones. Now, you can focus on what's ahead of you, and not what's behind you.

☐73. "Death cannot be conquered by man, but everything else in your path, kill it. Today, you were blessed with another 24 hours to conquer everything in your path. Don't avoid the challenge, for your reward is more in the trial than in the triumph. When I say your reward is in the trial, I mean that you get stronger in the journey that comes with facing a challenge."

We all have an expiration date; it's inevitable in this world. The key is to not live in the safe zone. The key is doing what makes you happy, inspiring others, and spreading love and kindness, not hate and fear. In doing so, you will feel better about yourself and make others feel good as well. As the human race, we are all held responsible for leaving the world a better place than it was when we came in. If we all do our part, the potential for this world is great. So, let the kindness start with you today.

☐74. "Don't avoid pain. In embracing pain, you are choosing to get out of your comfort zone. Nothing grows in your comfort zone; it's a safety net. Get out of the safety net, and go further than you have ever gone."

Comfort zones are for content people, people who are satisfied with their job, their income, their place of residence, and their overall lifestyle. There aren't too many people who feel that way. Who really doesn't want a better life? Well, it doesn't happen by chance, or by wishing it to magically happen. Failure is a tricky situation. The feeling of failure creates a bigger desire to succeed, and with that, you start to stretch your comfort zone and see how much further you can really go.

☐75. **"There is no shortcut to your dream. If there is, it won't last. The dream you are seeking is seeking you. Keep speaking it into existence, and make the necessary sacrifices to achieve it."**

Trust me, we all want the easy route to whatever it is we love and want out of life, but in reality we all know that if that happens, we either won't appreciate it, it won't last, or we will just take it for granted. Why do you think athletes cry when they win a championship, or when they get drafted? It's all because of the work they had to put in just to get to that point. Keep going after your dream! If it's easy, then it's not worth it. What you want has more value when you have to respect it and embrace the grind. Mentally, keep speaking as if you have it, and in the physical, the signs will start to appear.

☐76. **"Establish a foundation of people who hold you accountable and allow you to do the same for them. Stop hanging out with the 'seriously not serious' people."**

Too many of us have associates or people we hang out with who bring no value to our lives. These are the people you have nothing in common with, as far as from a business or success standpoint. You need people to hold you responsible, you do not need those who will make excuses for you as to why you did not finish a task or accomplish any goals.

☐77. **"Things won't happen when you think they should. Don't worry about that, keep on pushing, keep being persistent, and stay positive. However old you are right now, it took years to get there. You didn't get there overnight, so don't expect your dream to happen like that, either; it's a process."**

Success is not an overnight mission, it may not happen in a month or one year, but don't worry about how long it takes to get to your goal. You have to continuously push through, knowing every day you are getting closer. A baby doesn't walk right out of the womb; instead, it is a process where the baby must develop the strength to sit up, crawl, and then eventually walk. During those stages, the baby falls repeatedly, trying to sit up. Sometimes, the baby crawls backwards, trying to go forward, and the baby falls, trying to walk. It's all a process, but the baby keeps going and eventually walks. Then, they gain the confidence to run. It is okay to fail, but to fall and stay down is unacceptable! Get up and keep going.

Observing, Learning, and Applying

Week 12:

☐78. **"Every time you step outside, you are giving a first impression to somebody. You never know who that somebody is, or what they might be able to do for you. Keep that in mind when you think about frowning or being rude."**

We as people tend to wear our emotions on our sleeves and easily let people know that something is going wrong in our lives. We have to be able to not let what we are going through affect our everyday life; a bad attitude only prevents you from pursuing or embracing an opportunity. People really will decide not to help you based on your facial expressions. My mother would always tell me, "You get more bees with honey." Smile more often. Smiling and laughing are contagious behaviors, so pass it on.

☐79. **"Don't let someone else's opinion of you become your reality."**

Too many times, we allow what people think of us to determine how we live our lives. You cannot live your life for someone else. For example, people always want to give you advice, but as soon as that advice goes wrong, they will say, "I didn't make you do it!" and they are right. They didn't make you do anything; you just followed their advice. You are the only one who truly knows your situation. Have a mind of your own, live your life how you want to live it, and make sure if you get into trouble, it's because you chose to take the risk. Don't get in trouble following the pack or trying to fit in; there are enough followers in the world, and we need more leaders.

☐80. "Look at your circle of friends and associates, see if their goals align with your goals. Now, make a decision."

People will cut you off for no reason and you won't even know it. You need to stop holding onto dead weight. You are trying to go someplace in life, and if the people you associate with don't share the same vision, values, or principles, you are in trouble. Either you are going to hang out with them and stop pursuing your dream because of their unsupportive influence, or you will show love from a distance. If they don't understand, they were never your real friend, anyway.

☐81. "It doesn't cost to pay attention, shut up and listen."

It's that simple, shut up sometime. Even if you already know the answer, you don't have to respond. Some situations test your maturity level by testing how you respond, and the best response can be keeping your mouth closed. Listening, on the other hand, is a good thing because everyone loves a listener; listeners are easy to talk to, whether what's being said is relevant or not. You can learn a lot by listening. That's why we have two ears and one mouth, talk less and listen more.

☐82. "People want a Floyd Mayweather lifestyle and paycheck, but they don't have a Floyd Mayweather work ethic. Change your work ethic, and your lifestyle will follow."

What you have now is based on how hard you have worked in the past. How hard you are working now will determine what kind of benefits you see in the future. If you are tired of seeing mediocre results, create a more intensified work ethic for yourself. Professional boxer, Floyd Mayweather, works hard all of the time. If he goes to the club, he may jog 5 miles after. He doesn't drink or smoke, and he punches the speed bag for 45 minutes nonstop. That type of work ethic is nothing but a recipe for success.

☐83. **"Today, you will reap the rewards of the work you put in yesterday. How big the reward will be is up to you."**

You will benefit from your work in some shape or form, that's a promise. It may not be exactly what you want, but you will see change. The harder you work, the more successful you can become.

☐84. **"We have no way of knowing what's ahead of us in our future. All we can do is use what we have to make the best decision possible."**

You don't know what the future holds, so you can't try to put things off in the future. That business you want to start, that degree you want to have, the time to start is now. There is no longer a place for you to say, "I will do it later." You don't want to be in the same place you were in yesterday; that's not progress.

Sacrifice and Discipline

Week 13:

☐ 85. **"Today, sacrifice something that is hindering you from success. It may be 30 minutes of TV, it may be your social networks, or it may be pointless phone conversations. Watch how much more you get done when you eliminate the distractions. Each week subtract a distraction, and watch the progress you make."**

Sacrifice those distractions; they are stunting your growth. If it does not bring you closer to your goals, you shouldn't be doing it, and it's time to let it go. Discipline is supposed to be difficult, so don't look at what you don't get to do anymore, look at how it is going to allow you to be more successful.

☐ 86. **"Embrace not knowing the outcome of your struggle. And when you get a little alone time, look back on all you have been through during that period of time. If you happen to smile, that lets you know it was worth it."**

We will never know the outcome of our struggle; we don't even know if we can get through it. But one thing for sure, if you don't fight for it, you definitely won't get through it. Not knowing can be a great thing. Before you reach success, there will be bright spots here and there to let you know that you are on the right path. It is those moments that will keep you going.

☐ 87. **"Today is the day that you will start making decisions for lifetime results, not short-term resolutions."**

Too often, we make choices based on short-term or overnight success instead of sacrificing for the future and making sure we leave a good legacy behind. We have to stop being selfish by making moves for immediate results. Instead, we need to be willing to set ourselves up for the long term by putting in the hard work day in and day out. Shoot for lifetime happiness, not temporary enjoyment.

☐88. **"There is a new struggle every day, but you have to keep holding on."**

Each day brings a new challenge, whether it's big or small. Don't get it twisted: there will be a challenge either way. Life is about progression, and the only way to progress is to go through trials and tribulations. Don't try to avoid the battles because they are necessary to test your character and your strength. It is the trying times that allow you to grow in the midst of your journey.

☐89. **"Until you see yourself becoming something you are not, you won't be successful. That's called vision. You can't see yourself in the same place a year from today and think that's a recipe for success. Where you are right now is temporary, you won't be there for the rest of your life."**

Your current circumstances depend on your attitude and your willingness to change your life for the better. See yourself in the future and get a clear understanding of where you want to be in life. In addition, understand that it won't come by wishing, hoping, or talking. It will come by working hard, sacrificing, and enduring whatever comes your way. You can do it!

☐90. **"Wake up every day with excitement, knowing that your current circumstances are only temporary."**

Today is a great day, and so is every day after. Even if things aren't going right, it's still a good day. The day you don't wake up is the day you can't complain, and you can't do anything to fix *that* situation. Until that last day, you still have the power and the opportunity to do something about your current situation.

☐91. **"Find another reason besides money for why you do what you do, and watch the money come."**

How much money is enough money for you? You probably can't answer that question because money is something you can never really get enough of. We always want more, which is greedy. Do what you love because the money will only satisfy you for so long. Often, we see celebrities and icons resort to suicide. That's due to unhappiness, and most of them don't have money problems. Chase happiness, not a check.

Ask yourself, "Is it really in me?"

Week 14:

☐92. **"Turn your alarm clock off and see how much you really love what you do. If you can't get up and go to work without an alarm clock, change your profession. The love for what you do should wake you up."**

Waking up shouldn't be a problem, if you are doing what you love. At the end of the day, you should be *mad* that you have to go to sleep; you should want to spend every moment you can doing what you love. Let love and passion wake you up. Let love and passion be your alarm clock.

☐93. **"You are not going to go far in life by being selfish; share all you have, and in return, it may not be money, but watch the opportunities present themselves."**

You have so much to offer, but you are so stuck on what *you* need, or what you think you need, that you are acting selfishly. By being selfish, you are forfeiting opportunities, connections, and relationships that you don't even know exist. Share some of the things you possess and watch how it comes back to you. You will be amazed, and you will feel good for lending a helping hand.

☐94. **"The question is not how much you have to sacrifice—or what you have to sacrifice—to invest in your dream. The question is, are you willing to risk whatever it takes?"**

Too often, we try to calculate what it takes and how long it will take to get to our dreams and our goals. Honestly, if you knew how many hours a day and how many years it took to reach your goal, would you still do it? Probably not. Whatever you are working towards, be in it for the long haul. Stop worrying about the destination and how long it will take to get there, enjoy the journey.

☐ 95. "What everybody else tells you, 'no'. What you have to tell yourself, 'yes'."

In striving towards your goals and your dreams, you will hear the word "no" countless times. You can't let that deter you or overwhelm you. Use the word "no" as fuel to drive you until you reach a "yes". The love you have for your dreams and your goals allows you to endure the many "no's" in pursuit of a "yes".

☐ 96. "Some things in life you can't do anything about. Accept that and move on. Control what you can control."

In a lot of situations, life just happens; you don't know why things happen and you never will, so stop trying to figure out why. Fix what you can fix and move on. Don't dwell on what's out of your control because it's just that, out of your control. No matter what, be positive about everything and negative about nothing.

☐ 97. "You have to be willing to give up what you have in order to get to better. You may question it, but in the long run, you will understand."

You will have to eliminate in order to elevate and to accomplish whatever it is you want to accomplish in life. To lose weight, eliminate some foods; to relieve stress, eliminate a job or a relationship; to start a business, eliminate going out too much and taking time away from your business. When you want better for your life, it requires sacrifice; you have to be willing to dish it out in order to achieve success.

☐98. "You don't feel like waking up, huh? So what, who does? Get up and grind."

You complain about waking up. On average, most people wake up between 6am and 7am. But to get to where you want to go in life that requires you to *not* be average. The CEO of Pepsi wakes up at 4am, and the CEO of Disney wakes up at 4:30am. They are no different from you, except for the fact that they use their time wisely. If you don't use your time wisely, you will continue to be average because you would obviously rather rest than grind. And 9 times out of 10, you will probably rest for the wrong reason. Stop resting because you are tired, and rest only when you need it.

Get out of your own way

Week 15:

☐ 99. **"Your haters aren't the problem, it's you. Stop using them as an excuse for why you aren't moving forward."**

Haters significantly dislike you and everything about you. Now, please tell me how that affects your production. It doesn't! So, focus on the task, and not the people who dislike you. The only thing they have control over is how they feel about you, which should have no bearings on your actions. Keep moving!

☐ 100. **"The person you are today will not get you to your dreams of tomorrow. You have to grow every day. You have to be able to accept criticism, whether you agree or not."**

Wherever it is you see yourself in the future, you can't get there in one day. It is all about daily progression. With each passing day, you should be doing something to get closer to your goal. Criticism comes from every angle; you have to learn how to accept it. Don't let it avert you from your quest for success.

☐ 101. **"Life is good when you can look in the mirror and see what you've always dreamed of. Do what you have to do to gain that feeling."**

Life is not about going to a job you think about quitting every day. It's about waking up and doing what you love. In the process, use your success to guide people who want to do the same thing you are doing. If you don't have that feeling yet, don't worry. Whenever you get serious about self-happiness, look in the mirror and make a change.

☐ **102. "Don't let others try to persuade you otherwise because things didn't work out for them."**

Too often, we let others have too big of an influence on the decisions we make, and that's where we go wrong. People don't mean to doubt you, or make you feel uncertain with what you want to do, sometimes they are just scared for you, and that's fine. You must be able make decisions on your own. There is nothing wrong with listening to advice, but at the end of the day, follow your heart and not the words of someone who won't have to deal with the consequences of your decision.

☐ **103. "You will never hit the jackpot without putting coins in the machine. Invest in yourself until you hit the jackpot."**

Now, your jackpot may not be money; it may be a healthy relationship, a healthy body, or a new focus on your dreams. But whatever it is, invest in it and put coins in your machine. Too often, we want success without the hard work. We look at successful people and instantly see their achievements and want it, not knowing what they went through to get to where they are now. Stop wanting the shine without the grind because it just doesn't work like that.

☐ **104. "Chase your dream. Even if you don't reach it, there is a chance you will find something else you love in pursuit of it."**

Chasing a dream you have not yet accomplished requires getting out of your comfort zone, which in turn opens you up to another level of perseverance, sacrifice, and motivation.

With that transition, you develop a new confidence and discover who you really are. Once you find out more about yourself, you tend find other things that interest you as well; that's called growth. Don't be scared of it, embrace it.

☐ **105. "Most of you avoid pain, but in order to grow you must be able to endure pain. On the other side of pain is progress. With each level of pain you face, you get stronger in some aspect in your life, whether it is physically, mentally, or emotionally."**

Pain is weakness leaving the body, and it creates more room for growth. The more you experience, the tougher you become. Each trial you overcome is your own prerequisite to the next step of achieving whatever it is you are in pursuit of. Those trials develop you physically, mentally, and emotionally. Stop avoiding pain and take it head on.

A little reality check

Week 16:

☐ **106. "If you only do what you know how to do, you will never grow; that's a comfort zone. A comfort zone is an okay place for a person with no goals, but nothing ever grows there; you stay the same and develop complacency.**

Step out of your comfort zone and take leaps of faith. You may fall and get bumps and bruises, but you will also discover things about yourself you didn't even know. You are worth your own risk. Get away from complacency and embrace the challenges.

☐ **107. "Face the fact that things in life will not always be logical. There will be things that happen in life that cannot be explained."**

With some things, you will just not be able to piece together the whole puzzle, and that's fine. Just try to find the positives throughout the whole ordeal. Keep people around you who will push you to get through the hard times.

☐ **108. "When you are negative, you attract negative energy. Be positive and watch the positive energy flow. You have to be positive in negative situations."**

It's hard for you to be positive in a world full of negativity, but that's what separates the successful people from the average people. Average people can be positive sometimes, and when things get bad, they start doubting, questioning, and displaying a negative state of mind. Successful people encounter a bad or overwhelming situation and see another challenge, and a chance to prove others wrong. They see the positivity in everything. Negativity exists in the mind; get it out of there.

☐109. **"If you want to keep getting what you are getting, keep doing what you are doing. If you want different results, change the way you move, change what you listen to, change who you talk to, and most importantly, change your work ethic.**

Change starts with yourself, first and foremost. In order to get to place you have never gone, you have to do some things that you have never done before. In order to do that, your daily, weekly, monthly, and yearly routines have to change. You must make more sacrifices, make less excuses, and you must not blame others for your mistakes. Get to work!

☐110. **"You only get one life, do what you want with it. Stop letting the left hook of life hit you and make you throw in the towel. Keep fighting! Smooth seawater didn't make a great sailor, but the storms he or she overcame did."**

Life is tough, it hits hard with the loss of loved ones, the loss of jobs, unhealthy marriages and relationships, and the list goes on. With all of that being said, life's struggles help develop you into a strong human being, allowing you to share your wisdom with someone else who may be going through what you already preserved through. However, if you throw in the towel on life, you'll never know how it could've all turned out. Don't give up on yourself; you never know who is watching, and who is cheering you on.

☐ **111. "Today, be nice to everyone, even the people you dislike. You never know, you could save someone's life. Dish out positivity and watch it come back."**

Stop being selfish! Your life is not about you, as crazy as that might sound. It's very easy to make yourself happy, try making someone else's day and you might have just saved a life. You never know. Your words and actions go further than you could have ever imagined.

☐ **112. "You are not a product of your environment; that's something society has told us, and we believed it. You are a product of your work ethic. Whatever effort you put into whatever it is you do will determine the results you get back."**

TV, celebrities, and music all give us a false perception of life and what to think. We can't continue to let those things influence us, and at the end of the day, it is only enslaving our bodies and our minds. We are capable of obtaining everything our hearts' desire, but we must work extremely hard for it and treat people with respect along the way.

Go, go, go!

Week 17:

☐ 113. **"Find yourself waking up each day more confident than the last; this will be because of who you are becoming as a person, and who you are associating with."**

Be happy with the person you see yourself becoming, wake up excited to get on your grind, knowing each day that you are improving and becoming the best "you" that you can become. Everyone else is taken, be yourself.

☐ 114. **"Nobody can do what you do as good as you can do it. Get your focus up. Your vision was given to you, not to anyone else. Don't worry about why they don't understand what you're trying to do."**

You are great at something, find out what it is! Place your focus on it in order to perfect it and turn it into a profit. In doing so, you will find yourself doing what you love and what you are great at for the rest of your life. It will never feel like "work" ever again. Whatever your vision is, act on it. People may not understand the situation, but it's not for them; it's for you, remember that.

☐ 115. **"You don't have to be very talented. You may be average or a little above average in talent. Where you have to excel is with your work ethic, plain and simple. Trust me, everything else will fall in place."**

Everyone is born with some sort of talent, but very few get by with just talent alone. In order to be great, you must have an intense work ethic. Work ethic will take you places only talent can dream of. Work hard in everything you do, but most of all, work hard consistently, not just sometimes.

☐ 116. "Live in service to others more than in service to yourself, meaning if you do not produce, others will suffer."

People are depending on you to survive, whether it's your family, your friends, or society in general. Do not stunt their growth because you don't want to work hard. Give back what you have gained, whether it is financially, physically, spiritually, or emotionally. We are all placed in roles that will allow us to help make the world a better place.

☐ 117. "Stop looking at how far away the end goal is, that's where you mess up and start to question yourself. You must start one step at a time and walk as straight as you can. Every now and then, look over your shoulder to see how far you have come; that is the true measure of success."

Too often, we get blinded by how far we have to go, which starts to draw in doubt and uncertainty. Keep focusing on the next step—not the next ten—because you can't get there until you get past the current position you are in. It's okay to look back in order to give yourself some encouragement to solider on, and for you to see how far you have come and to see the troubles you have conquered.

☐ 118. "You have to be willing to do what is required. Your motivation may be poverty, or people telling you that you can't, or even the loss of a family member. Everyone has something that pushes them; find out what motivates you and use that when the times get

tough. Make that reason the driving force behind why you do what you do."

Everyone is motivated by different things: money, the struggle, or family problems. Whatever your motivation is, write it down. Post pictures in a place that allows you to look at it or read it every day. Use that motivation to get you through each day, each trial, and each problem as they come. Your reason for why you do what you do will take you a long way.

☐ **119. "Calculate all of your free time and add it up for a week. When I say 'free time', I mean the time spent playing video games, going to the club, watching TV, and the time spent on pointless text and phone conversations."**

Use those hours to write that book you want to write, to start that business you want to open, or to go back to school so you can get another job. But sacrifice the idle time for a positive benefit. Stop wasting time on activities that do not allow you to grow. Use your time wisely.

Appreciate the process

Week 18:

☐ 120. **"Do not wear your feelings on your sleeve, some people love to see when things are going wrong. Don't give them the satisfaction."**

Your facial expressions give away clues of what you are going through. As a result, you have to be careful with what you show to the public. Some people like to see when other people are unhappy, so keep a smile on your face, and never let them know when you are hurting.

☐ 121. **"The truth is opportunities don't just knock once; you just have to make sure you are ready the second time around if you blew the first opportunity."**

You will get opportunities if you continue to work. If you don't work, opportunities won't find you. Don't forfeit an opportunity by choosing to not work because if you aren't working, how can you be ready for the opportunity when it finally presents itself? You can't, so keep working! Someone is always watching. Keep the opportunities coming.

☐ 122. **"Cherish the present no matter what the circumstances are. You are not promised tomorrow, so make the best of today. Today is all you have, and the past was all you were promised."**

You may be going through tough times, but there are people who aren't alive who would've rather lived through those tough times you are facing now than to be gone from earth. We only have the present, and that's all that should be on your mind. Treat people well while you can, and lend out a helping hand. Kindness can be contagious.

☐123. **"One of the hardest things in life is learning to take it one day at a time; we all spend so much time planning for the future and end up messing it up by not enjoying the present. Enjoy today, tomorrow isn't promised."**

Maybe a year or so ago you worked hard to get where you are right now. Yes, you want a better future—we all do—but tomorrow isn't promised. Enjoy all that you have already worked for, but still continue to work hard for the future. You don't want to work so hard and so much that you forget to live and enjoy.

☐124. **"Focus on your grind and let others focus on the weekends, the summers, and the holidays."**

Many average people focus on how they are going to spend their off time, you should not include yourself in that bunch. The reason why is because your dreams and your goals aren't average, so you can't do what they do. There's nothing wrong with average people and what they do, but that's not what you are working so hard to become. Separate yourself through the sacrifices you willingly make and through your work ethic.

☐125. **"Today, learn from every situation you face. There is no education like learning from and through adversity."**

Today, you will have to make tough decisions. The decisions you make will be both small and big, and the outcome may bring unwanted stress and tension. However, make sure that you learn something from the situation. Don't come out of the situation dumbfounded because you may find yourself facing the same problem in the future—and if possible—you want to avoid making the same mistakes. Encounter each situation as an opportunity to gain more knowledge to do better later on.

☐ **126. "The failures you face are just the beginning stages of success. The failures don't mean turn around, they mean, 'Just not yet'."**

If you are expecting to fail, just go ahead and stop. Save yourself the headache. If you aren't willing to invest your last dollar, your last bit of energy, or your sleepless nights on a continuous basis, don't bother. The road to success is not an overnight deal. Nobody knows how long it takes to reach success, but they endure the grind. NBA superstars knew at a young age that they wanted to play in the NBA, but it couldn't happen when they were 9 years old; they had to go through high school, college, and some took even longer and unconventional routes to get there. All in all, that's years of training, failing, and resiliency. Be resilient.

Keep a positive mindset!

Week 19:

☐ **127. "Today, with all the negativity going around, be that positive vibe."**

If it's not positive, don't say it, don't think it, and don't act on it. Run away from negativity that hinders you from being successful, and run away from people who won't help you. Negativity attracts negative vibes, and vice versa. Hear, speak, and act positively.

☐ **128. "Who said opportunity knocks once? Just be ready the next time."**

Be careful of the opportunities you forfeit, whether it's by choice or simply because you weren't ready. Too many people are killing for the opportunities that you are passing by, so you better take the next one and run with it, or be left empty-handed.

☐ **129. "There is no slowing down, you have to keep going. Everything takes time. You have to believe that everything will be all right."**

You have been working hard. You're almost there, so don't give up now, and keep pushing. Keep speaking positively to yourself, and listen to inspirational music and motivators. You don't need anything that's only going to make you question what you are doing.

☐130. **"Help people when you can. The shoe always has a chance of being on the opposite foot sooner or later down the line."**

Never do anything in hopes of getting something in return; that's not genuine. If you do anything, do it because it's the right thing to do. If you have it, share it. Don't be so selfish that you have more than enough, and your neighbor is there with nothing.

☐131. **"Stop being ready to shine before the grind, it doesn't work like that."**

Too often, we look at the TV and we see instant success, and we want it for ourselves in the quickest way possible. In reality, the only way to get it that quickly is to hit the lottery. So, unless you are sure you are going to win, get on your grind.

☐132. **"Every time you doubt your dream, you kill it slowly. Nobody else but you can do that. You aren't here to doubt yourself, let everybody else do that."**

The only person who can truly deter you from your dreams and your goals is you. Yes, people may talk negatively, but that's all that it is, talk. Don't let that get to you. A majority of the time, those same people wish they were in your shoes or had your opportunity.

☐133. **"Everything is going to be all right, what you are going through is just all in your mind."**

A lot of the time, we create problems that really aren't even there. It may not be that you want to deal with the problem, but you create more work for yourself than is necessary just by overthinking or overanalyzing something. Be careful what you let influence you, the mind is tricky and powerful.

It's on you

Week 20:

☐ **134. "Today, you may wake up and complain about aches, pains, and problems. Get up. Is your heart still beating? Is there is a roof over your head? Then go grind!"**

Now ask yourself, "Why aren't I smiling?" Things could be so much worse than what they are. I am sure you personally know some people who have it a thousand times worse than you. Did you see that family on the news whose house burned down? The story on the family with the missing child? Or that woman who was found dead in the park? How bad are you doing now?

☐ **135. "Your mama said, your daddy said, your friends said, your boss said, your coaches said...man, forget what they *said*! What are you going to *do*?"**

Everyone will have an opinion on what you should do with your life based on their own mistakes. This is your life; you live it the way you want to and you decide what you want to do. They can live with your regrets, and so can you. Make your own choices when it comes to your life. Their opinion is not your reality.

☐ **136. "You have a greater purpose than to just be here on earth. We all are responsible for making the world a better place. Do something today to make an impact on the world and leave your mark."**

Yes, you have a job and there's nothing wrong with doing what you do, but do not limit your life only to that one specific job. We all are blessed with gifts and talents that can help someone else become great. Don't die with your greatness stuck inside you; leave the world something it can use in a constructive and positive manner.

☐137. **"Don't you ever get *too* comfortable; someone else is working hard for that spot you have. You better not take it for granted."**

It isn't hard to become comfortable with something, especially if you worked really hard for it. But the key to maintaining success is striving for more and embracing more challenges. Don't you ever think that you are irreplaceable in anything you do because you *are*.

☐138. **"Look around, either you love what you have or you want better. The key to maintaining what you have and obtaining more is working harder and working consistently."**

Contentment is a disease, and it's contagious. Don't be satisfied with your life, even if you have all of your desires. In obtaining all of your desires, there comes a responsibility to maintain them, and that requires work. In order to obtain your desires, you must create a tough work ethic and sustain it throughout your journey. Adversity will be there either way, and that's what you have to overcome.

☐139. **"To stay where you are, be consistent in what you are already doing. To move on to bigger and better things, work harder consistently."**

Consistency is a challenge, and it requires you to do something out of the norm in order to better yourself. Don't get it twisted; you can be consistent at not trying and giving up. Examine the things you have developed a consistent attitude and behavior towards.

☐ **140. "You may be going through it, that's life. Everyone has trials, but survive today by pushing through."**

Know that you *do* matter in this world, so don't give up. Your breakthrough is so close, and we know this because you are breaking down. The closer you get to coming out of the storm, the harder things tend to get. Keep pushing, keep striving, and keep going!

Life keeps going, so should you

Week 21:

☐141. "'Settled', 'content', 'complacent', 'relaxed', and 'comfortable' are all words that mean you will be in the same spot next year that you are currently in now. If the people around you have those traits, it's time to love them from a distance."

When people say, "Man, you are acting brand new!" That's fine because you are changing to better yourself. The actual tragedy is that they are staying the same, and life is passing them by. The only person you can control is you, so do what you have to do. Examine who you associate with because they have a big influence on the activities you partake in.

☐142. "Who am I, or anybody else for that matter, to tell you what you can and can't do? The answer is nobody. Remember that when someone doubts you or tells you that you can't."

In life, there will be plenty of people who will tell you what you can and can't do based on the experiences that they have had. They will tell you this out of fear for you and out of hatred for your soon-to-come success. You have to learn how to separate yourself from those people. As long as they are around, they will keep you at their level or underneath them. If they really had your best interests at heart, they would support you in whatever it is you decide to do. Keep your head up, keep your eyes open, and remain locked in on what you have going on.

☐143. "Stay focused on today, don't let distractions distract you."

Too often, we will find ourselves on a roll in all aspects of our lives: financially, relationship wise, and with our achievements. All it takes is one little distraction to knock your focus off; you can't let that happen because more often than not, it's harder to get back on track than it is to keep running in stride with the momentum you had before you were distracted. Remain focused on being focused and eliminate those distractions.

☐144. "Stop saying that if you knew what you knew now, you would have done things differently."

That's the case for everyone. Unfortunately, you nor myself can go back and change the past. We only have the future to work with, and we must deal with what's ahead. We all have regrets, and we all have to be mature enough to face the consequences of our actions. Even though you made a decision you think you regret, some of those choices have in turn led you to other decisions that you are very proud of. The key is to learn from the regrets and to never make the same mistake twice. As long as you are able to live with your decisions, it really wasn't right or wrong because the right decision could have had the wrong outcome, and vice versa.

☐145. "The fact that you are still here means you can still get better. You can still give, receive, and apply more to your life."

It's not a coincidence that you wake up every day, but don't take it for granted because you aren't promised tomorrow. Achieve all of your heart's desires, and help as many people as you can without expecting anything in return. Remove pride from your ways; nobody likes a prideful person. Be humble, selfless, and respectful. In doing that, you will better yourself, and in the midst of that, you can make someone else's life better in the process.

☐146. "Wake up today and do whatever it takes, so you won't be stuck tomorrow asking, 'What if?'"

It's better to live a life full of attempts than a life full of wondering, "What if?" Whatever it takes to better your life, you have to be willing to do it, or you will remain where you are in life. It's your choice, but the world won't stop for you.

☐147. "Your yesterdays are prerequisites for your tomorrows. With that being said, don't waste today; you will be left behind tomorrow. The world won't stop moving for you, so don't stop moving for anything in the world."

Success is not easy; it takes time. There are no overnight successful businesses, doctors, athletes, singers, actresses, or lawyers, and the list goes on. Everyone has to put in their time and pay their dues. The dues you paid in the past paved the way for where you are now. If you are not happy with it, you need to put in more time and work harder to reap better benefits the next go round. Again, success is not easy. That's why everyone isn't successful.

Welcome the challenges with open arms

Week 22:

☐**148. "The only difference between the successful people and the unsuccessful people is the word 'no'. To successful people 'no' means, 'Try again', to unsuccessful people, it means, 'I can't do it'."**

You have to be willing to try over and over again until you get it right. Yes, you may fail, but each time you fail, you are learning and getting closer and closer to achievement. An above average hit rate for a baseball player is 300, that's *above* average. That means out of 10 times at bat, he hits the ball at least 3 times. He has failed 7 times, but he is still a millionaire. What you need to understand is that your failures won't define you. Instead, the effort and the amount of adversity you have faced will instill new characteristics in you. It is *those* characteristics that will define you.

☐**149. "You are either going *into* a storm, going *through* a storm, or on your way *out* of one."**

Tough times, nobody likes them, but from the day you were born you have had them. As a newborn, it's a tough world. No one really knows when you are hungry unless you cry, and no one really knows when you have to go to the bathroom until it smells. As a teenager, you are more able-bodied, but it's still a tough world as well. You have trouble making friends or you experience bullying. Young adults also have a tough task ahead of them in figuring out how to navigate the world on their own. Last but not least, adults have a tremendous responsibility—not only to themselves—but also to those around them, and to those who depend on them for guidance. Those are a few examples of the storms that we all have to overcome at each stage in our lives. Remember, storms are meant to teach you and make you better. Don't give up before it's over.

☐ **150. "Let the space between where you are in your life at this very moment and where you want to get to inspire you."**

Looking at how far it takes to get someplace can be discouraging because it may seem *too* far. Look at how far you have already come and what you have been through. Smile for the journey you have been through, knowing all that it took to get there. Now, get innovative on the rest of the journey ahead!

☐ **151. "If you want to get somewhere different, then do something different."**

Many people will go to the weight room and do the same routines over and over again. Meanwhile, their bodies never change, they only remain the same. Until you decide to challenge yourself, you will continue to be in the same spot, or even end up taking steps backwards. We all have the ability to be something other than what we are. But until you do something unfamiliar and unknown, you will continue to be stationary where you are.

☐ **152. "Drive and desire are the tools you need to accomplish your dreams and your goals because the journey is not for the weak. If you want it bad enough, you will do whatever it takes to get there. If not, you will continue to make excuses."**

A strong mentality and an even stronger work ethic are needed if you want to accomplish your goals. Everything starts with a vision of where you see yourself in the future, then you create a plan and discipline yourself to making it a habit and sticking with it. Once it's a habit, the hard part is over. This is why many people continue to work a job that they dislike; they've made it a habit, and they are now paying their dues. The same goes for your dream; pay your dues, and reap the benefits later.

☐ 153. "Don't let success defeat you."

You have won some major battles in your life, and you will continue to win, relationship wise, athletically, and financially. The key is to not get big headed and think that you are better than anyone else. You must remember that you were not always at a good point in your life. You only just got there. As quickly as you got it, you can lose it. Humility, do you have it?

☐ 154. "Be able to adapt to your environment. Don't get comfortable, and know the difference."

Adapting to your environment does not mean you have to go through all of the necessary changes to make sure everything is good for you, but it does mean that you must adjust to the environment you are in as much as possible, so you won't be miserable or unsatisfied. Being comfortable is a sense of normality, while adapting to different situations is challenging because change is needed. Nothing grows in that comfort zone because that is only sticking to what you know. What's the challenge in that?

Time and Effort

Week 23:

☐ **155. "One of the most valuable things you have on this earth is time."**

You have to use your time more wisely. When your time on this earth is done, how do you want to be remembered? Do not answer that question by your words, answer it by your actions. Commit to carrying out more selfless acts, make others smile, and sacrifice your comfort for someone else's blessing.

☐ **156. "Your thoughts become your actions, especially when you start acting on those thoughts as if you already have it."**

If you consistently think things aren't going to work out in your favor, they won't. Until you change your mindset to be more positive, no matter what the circumstances may be, you will keep getting disappointing results. Also, just because you think positively doesn't mean you don't have to work. Don't get it twisted; the people you look up to or admire didn't get there off of pure vision without putting the hard work in. Start with your thinking, and then fuel that tank with your effort.

☐ **157. "Don't be a, 'One day I'm going to' person."**

That's a person you don't want to become. One day I'm going to lose weight, one day I'm going to start my own business, one day I'm going to go back to school and get my degree. I don't know about you, but I wasn't promised tomorrow. With that being said, you have to accomplish all you can *today*. You can't be a dreamer all of your life; you have to eventually wake up and start chasing your dreams.

☐ **158. "There are never zero problems or free moments, something will always come up."**

Now that you know this, there is no excuse for why you can't do something, or why you are not doing what you love. I just told you that you will endure adversity, so it is up to you whether or not you want to overcome it.

☐ **159. "Nobody wants to hang around a low energy, negative-minded, and unmotivated individual."**

Become that person who everyone likes to be around; that person is one who brings life, positivity, and happiness. Nobody wants to start a business with a person who complains all of the time. Create someone else's happiness. All of that starts with *your* attitude.

☐ **160. "Yes, good things might come for those who wait, but those opportunities came from those who hustled and turned them down."**

You better stop waiting on that opportunity and go create one for yourself. You are the author of your own book. You may not be able to control all of the chapters exactly like you want to, but you *can* control the direction you want your book go in.

☐ **161. "Today, be your best, regardless of your past and current circumstances."**

Your past doesn't define you, and don't let your present moments control you. Change the way you think, and think positively for positive expectations. You should only be looking forward because that's where your life is headed; everything that is behind you is just that, behind you. It's time for you to get over the past. Move on because success is ahead and waiting on you.

Courage and Obedience

Week 24:

☐ 162. "Today, don't let the world tell you all that you are not. Instead, look in the mirror and tell yourself all that you are and all that you will become."

It can start with something as simple as turning on the news and seeing racism on TV. Something as small as that can discourage you from doing something you want to achieve. Society has a way of sending messages about how we can't be successful without a degree, how we don't have the ability to play a sport, and how we can't be good actors or good singers. Don't let that get to you; you are more than a conqueror. Anything you want, you can achieve. It will require work, though. That's a promise.

☐ 163. "Better slow and right, than fast and wrong."

Too often, we want things quickly. The packages we order, we want them shipped instantly overnight. With our food, we want it in a matter of minutes from the various fast food restaurants, or even out of a microwave. As a result, we have spoiled ourselves with how fast we want things because we have yet to realize that fast isn't always good. Your dream will not happen like that. I'm sorry to burst your bubble, but dreams require time, effort, work, patience, and sacrifice.

☐ 164. "The only person who can change your life is the person you see in the mirror today."

Others cannot create the happiness that you can create for yourself, so stop relying on other people to make you happy. When you look in the mirror, you should see yourself as a blessing to the world and to everyone you come in contact with. That's not arrogant, that's just understanding your worth. Don't let anyone make you feel any less about yourself. You are great, you are beautiful, you are lovable, you are worthy, you are appreciated, and you are everything you've ever wanted to be.

☐**165. "Your will to get better has to be bigger than your want for rest."**

Yes, we all get tired, but ask yourself, "Am I sleeping because I am tired from working hard, or am I sleeping from facing the obstacles of the day?" Google successful people, and you will see that the average human sleeps around 7 to 9 hours. Meanwhile, successful people will get about 5 to 6 hours of sleep. They often wake up at 3am or 4am to start their day. Be honest, some us don't go to bed until 2am or 3am, and we usually aren't doing anything productive until then. To a successful person, every hour they spend up and alert is an hour to be productive. It is the average person who needs breaks, naps, or days off. If you want better, you have to do better.

☐**166. "Don't get discouraged from practicing your craft, whatever it may be. Practice is only a lost art to those who can't or don't see the value in it."**

Too often, we get tired of going through the same process, even if it is to better ourselves. We may not see the transition, but it *is* happening. Where we mess up is when we allow ourselves to get distracted. It is then that we notice that others are doing something different from what we are doing, and that they are getting "better" results. Remember, it's a different stroke for different folks. In other words, everything isn't for everybody. Focus on that person you see in the mirror every day because that's the only person you can control.

☐ 167. "No step forward is too small, and a step back isn't always a digression."

In basketball, a step back can free you from a defender, so you are able to shoot the ball. That step back also allows you to create space from the defender to make a counter move for an easier or better shot. However, that step back doesn't just limit you to shooting; in taking a step back, you can also create room to do something else with the ball, such as pass the ball, which you couldn't do before you took a step back. Don't get discouraged by the baby steps; you have to crawl before you can walk. That step back is a great move because it allows you to see things from a different view.

☐ 168. "You have to gain the courage to start saying 'no' to the things that won't get you a 'yes'."

At times, we do things and wonder what's wrong with what we did. We wonder, "What harm is it doing to me?" The answer is that it's doing more harm than you can actually imagine. If it's not helping you get to where you want to go, why are you doing it? It is *hindering* you; that time spent doing something non-beneficial to what you are in pursuit of should be replaced with something that allows you to get closer to your dreams and your goals.

Let's talk about perspectives

Week 25:

☐169. **"In order to get to where you want to go, you have to stop hanging around people who don't have as much to lose as you do."**

You have to face the fact some of the people you grew up with are not on your level. They don't think like you do and they don't share the same values as you, and that is totally fine. We are all unique in our own ways. With that being said, you have more to lose and to sacrifice than they do because you are the only one who can invest in yourself. If they don't want what you want, you *have* to separate yourself from them and love them from a distance. For example, because they have a different vision than you do, the way you react in a situation can be completely different from the way they react in a situation. That difference in reaction could cost them nothing and cost you everything.

☐170. **"Discipline yourself to say 'no' to the things you like in order to reach the things you desire."**

For most people, it's so hard to accept the word "no", and it's hard to tell someone "no". You have to be able to embrace that word little by little and turn it into a, "Not yet". In addition, you have to be comfortable with telling people "no" and *not* feel the need to explain yourself. A majority of the time, we explain ourselves to sugarcoat the real reason we said "no" in the first place. If you have to accept the word "no" from others without it being sugarcoated, learn how to dish it out the same way.

☐171. **"If you weren't blessed with the ability to speak, what would your life say? What have you done for others that speaks volumes?"**

Anyone can say that they have done plenty of things for others, but what would people say about you that leaves a lasting impression? Make your actions speak louder than your words; show people instead of telling them. When you leave this life, leave all of your good deeds and your positive memories behind for others to remember. If you couldn't answer the question of what you did for others, I want your actions to eventually be able to answer that question. Let your answer speak from the work you've put in, and from the lives you've changed and affected in a positive manner.

☐172. **"The moment you get too high, life will humble you. At just the moment you get too low, life will crumble you. Try to be in the middle, just right."**

Don't expect or anticipate anything because if it doesn't reach your expectations, you are left disappointed. If you get too excited, or if you are too relaxed, you won't be ready for whatever happens. Everything will be a surprise and will happen too fast for you. But if you are just right, if you are excited just enough, you will be ready for whatever comes your way. The lights won't blind you and your opponent won't outshine you.

☐173. **"You can't want to be the best at anything and take days off. Each day, you have to do something to get better."**

It's plain and simple; the way you create a habit is by continuously doing the same thing over and over again for at least 21 days. To achieve what you want in life, you have to work towards it every day; there is no time off. By doing something to get better every day, you create a habit and a work ethic that allows you to push through when the times get tough, or when you feel like giving up and giving in.

☐ **174. "You can't spend more time planning your outfit than you spend planning to reach your dreams. Clothes won't make you successful."**

We are often too caught up in the latest fashion. To some, that's just a cover for how we really feel inside. We are hiding the pain of not being where we want to be in life. So, we think that by looking good people can't see that we are in fact unhappy. If you think about it, people often say, "I need to shop, I'm stressed out!" Well, shopping is a temporary enjoyment because it can only last for so long. When the initial high wears off, then you will need more clothes, which will only put you in the hole, especially if money is already tight to begin with. This is not the case for everyone, but a lot of people spend time planning for something that won't help make them successful. Spend more time doing what it takes to actually *make* you happy instead of using that time to buy things that make you *look* like you are happy.

☐ **175. "When you go out, it should be an act of celebrating an accomplishment, not just to celebrate, period. If you are not accomplishing anything in life, why are you celebrating?"**

You know people like this—and maybe you are one of them—the people who go out every weekend, spending money on things that don't really matter. Don't get it twisted, there's nothing wrong with going out, if you have everything in order and you can afford to. But if you are not where you should be financially, you should not feel comfortable going out that much. Some people go out every weekend just to celebrate that it's Friday, but the level that you want to reach doesn't require you to go out every Friday. Instead, it requires you to put extra hours in the gym, it requires you to spend extra time studying, or it requires you to put extra hours into that business proposal. You see, everybody can't get to where you want to go because they can't discipline themselves to put in the hours towards their dreams instead of putting in hours towards the bar or the club.

THOT = The Hustle Over Time

Week 26:

☐176. **"Don't get up thinking about chasing paper, focus on the purpose and the paper will chase you."**

There has to be a reason why you do what you do, and that reason has to be something other than money. Enough money is never really enough money, meaning you will never be satisfied with your income; you will always want more. Find something you love and chase it. Don't worry about the income. If you grind enough, the money will make its way to you. You have to stay true to eat. Don't cheat it, put in the overtime, but make sure you love it. When times get hard, your love will continue to push you forward.

☐177. **"Make a choice and stick with that decision. Don't judge yourself regardless of the outcome."**

We all make questionable decisions, and that's fine. You just have to be able to live with the outcome. Just because you made a decision and the results didn't come out like you planned doesn't mean you made the wrong decision. You'll never know what was on the other side. One thing for certain, you have clearly made the right decision because you are still alive. Stop beating yourself up over what you think are bad choices; beating yourself up won't change the decision or the outcome, it only clouds your mind for your next decision.

☐178. **"When you start to judge yourself, you bring in emotions. Emotional decisions are not good because most of the time regret always follows."**

You can't make too many decisions off of pure emotion. Just because someone made you upset leads to your bills not getting paid, or you just don't feel well, so nothing gets paid. Those types of emotional decisions are usually negative ones and can lead to regret. You have to put your problems to the side and make decisions with a clear and rational mind, regardless of what's going on in your life. Life hits everyone, but that is absolutely no reason to make emotional decisions. Be strong enough to take life's punches and continue to fight.

☐179. "That anger that you are holding onto is only hurting you. Nobody else will suffer, just you."

You're walking around pouting, being nasty, and having an over all bad disposition, which is only stunting your growth. The only person who can make you feel that way is yourself, unless you give other people that power over you. You are a great person! Now, you may not be where you want to be in life, but believe me, a lot of people aren't, either. Taking your problems out on others won't fix your problems, either. You may display a bad attitude around the wrong person, and that person might be the one who can help you get to where you want to go. All that means is you blew an opportunity. That negative attitude has already left you in the same spot for too long; try changing to see where a good attitude can take you.

☐180. "Humans are the only known species who make an excuse for why they don't eat, whether it's food or finances."

Does a starving lion wait or go hunt? Does a crocodile wait until you come *in* the water or will he chase you *out* of the water? Develop an animal instinct that forces you to take what you want. Stop thinking success is given away because it's not; success has a price, and the way the game is played is by paying for it. How you pay for it is by devoting hours and hours towards whatever it is you want to be successful at. Go out and take what's yours; it's time to eat.

☐ **181. "You might get lucky and get handed a degree, but chances are slim if you think people are just handing happiness out. Happiness has a price, are you willing to pay?"**

I'm not saying that this is the case for everyone, but some people can get through college easily without putting in any work. You have to be crazy to think success and happiness will come that easily as well. You have to be willing to put in the work needed to create your own happiness. Success isn't given; it's a 24/7 grind that will eventually lead you to success. Be willing to invest in your own happiness and success. If not, work for someone else who invested in theirs.

☐ **182. "You have to spend more time working on you, developing you, and finding out who you are in order to find out what truly makes you happy."**

We tend to spend a lot of time with other people, and in doing so, we prevent ourselves from discovering what we truly like. Until you are able to distance yourself from everything you know—environments, people, and influences—you won't know what you like and what makes you happy. We spend too much time trying to be liked, so we listen, watch, and act in certain ways in order to be liked by other individuals. Be liked by yourself!

Grind for something!

Week 27:

☐ **183. "Learn the difference between sleeping to renew your strength, and sleeping to avoid your challenges."**

It's a given that the human body needs sleep, but are you sleeping to be productive, or are you sleeping to avoid life? Sleeping will not change your situation; however, waking up and grinding for what you want will. Some people are broke and they are getting 8 to 10 hours of sleep. I'm going to be honest, you should not be sleeping that much. You are well rested and struggling, it just doesn't make sense. Cut out some of those hours of sleep and put them into a job, a second job, or a dream. Put those hours into something that equals productivity. If you aren't careful, you are only going to sleep your life away. Don't be mad at other people when you aren't where you want to be in life. Don't be mad at the people who made it because they woke up and got productive.

☐ **184. "When you start to wake up before the alarm clock, that's called purpose."**

The problem is that success hasn't become a habit for you, waking up early to do something towards your goals and dreams is non-existent, so you use an alarm clock. When you are pursuing something you love, that love and excitement is what wakes you up; you don't need an alarm clock. Success is a never-ending journey, you may achieve your goal and that's just reaching success, but sustaining it is a whole different level. See, when people become successful in something they don't love, they become complacent and stagnant. However, if you love it and reach success, you are still trying to find ways to expand, and you still have the same drive that you started with. No alarm clock is needed.

☐185. "Success is in the eye of the beholder. People say, 'Beauty is in the eye of the beholder,' and I believe that the same goes for success."

Nobody can tell you what success is. If your dream is to become a high school teacher, go win a Teacher of the Year award because you are a success. If you want to be a coach, achieve that goal because you are a success. Society tries to make us believe that success is all about money, nice houses, nice cars, and all of the other famous people we can associate with. That is false; whatever dreams you have that you achieve, that is a success. Don't try to live like these celebrities you see paraded in magazines. A majority of them are unhappy and don't have much of a choice. They can't do the things they really want to do because they have contracts to fulfill.

☐186. "Negative energy drains you, it takes too much to frown and to have an attitude. On the other hand, positive energy allows room for growth and opportunity."

Yes, we all have times where we are just not in the mood, or we don't want to be bothered. That's life, things happen and we have to be able to keep a positive outlook on the situation, no matter what. In the blink of an eye, your situation can go from bad to good. We must be optimistic and positive about every challenging situation.

☐187. "With each level of success, there comes a whole new level of challenges."

I hope you didn't think that once you *did* finally reach some of your goals that the challenges would stop. With each level of triumph, there is a new level of adversity. The key is having the ability to endure the struggle just as you have done in the past. No, it won't be the same; it will get tougher each time. Just like if you were lifting weights, you can do 4 reps of 10, but if after each set, you add 10 pounds, that makes the weight heavier and heavier. In the end, you become stronger, and you will continue to add more and more weight.

☐188. "You keep hollering about how there's not enough time in a day, that's because you are sleeping too much. Less sleeping equals more grinding."

Many people use the excuse, "I couldn't get to it because I didn't have enough time." Sometimes, that can be true, but then again ask yourself, "How many hours am I sleeping?" You think you need 8 hours to be productive simply because some scientist said so. Well, they also said that the world was ending in 2012. You have to create a new habit, a new normal for yourself. Obviously, what you are doing isn't working; you've been in the same place in life for quite some time now. But, it's time for a change. I promise you, take away 2 hours from your sleep and that's 14 more hours a week to be productive. What could you do with 14 more hours in a week? Don't worry; I know the answer, a lot!

☐189. "Today, be first and last. Be the first to get to work and the last to leave."

You want that promotion, but how are you setting yourself apart from everyone else? All jobs require you to put in a certain amount of hours per day, but if possible, put in more time to show yourself worthy of a pay raise or a position change. When you are working, you don't work for the job you have now, you work for the job you want. If you only do what is required, you will only get what is given. If you want more, then do more.

Overcoming the odds

Week 28:

☐190. **"One thing I know about you is that you have what it takes to *not* quit. The reason I know this is because this isn't the first page of this book, and you are still reading."**

You are not put into any situation to give up, no matter how challenging or overwhelming it may seem. In life, you will run into storms and some will be longer than others. You must have the ability to persevere through the tough times. Of course, it's not going to be easy, but the storms are there to make you a stronger individual. A lion wakes up every day hungry, knowing it has to catch the slowest gazelle. A gazelle wakes up every day, knowing it has to be able to outrun the fastest lion. Neither animal can quit; if the lion does, then he won't eat. If the gazelle quits, then he won't live. Don't quit, there's much more on the line than you think.

☐191. **"Don't be so afraid to fail that you don't allow yourself to attempt anything."**

There's nothing wrong at all with being a little nervous about anything, but never be too shaken up to try. The feeling of regret is worse than the feeling of not attempting and always wondering, "What if?' You can't let failure darken your vision because you will probably hear the word "no" a million times, but each "no" gets you closer to one "yes". Failure can be a part of your recipe for success; all you have to keep in mind is that perfection is not obtainable, but in the pursuit of perfection, greatness can be stumbled upon, even if being good was the only intent.

☐192. **"If you leave them with the inability to question your work ethic, you have the ability to accomplish anything."**

You will have plans and visions that only you can realize the impact they will have. But with your relentless drive, your effort, and the amount of time you put into it, you can slowly persuade people you have a masterpiece. If you are willing to put in the overtime it requires, then you pretty much have all of the confirmation you need, and more times than not, it becomes time for manifestation.

☐193. **"Plan, try, fail, grow, try again, fail, grow, try again, fail, grow, and try again. Soon, you won't keep failing."**

Just because you failed a couple of times doesn't make you a failure. It *does* make you a person who doesn't give up easily, and that is needed in the pursuit of your dreams and your goals. Too often, we think success comes easy or without a price. That it may come from looking at others and seeing what they have. However, we don't see what they had to go through in order to reap the benefits of their achievements. You don't have to change your dreams, just alter your plans. Some people need more alterations than others.

☐194. **"Fall *forward* because that's a step closer to where you are headed. It's a lot closer than falling backwards."**

When you think of falling, don't always think of it as a bad thing. Yes, at the time, it may be hard to understand why, but you may be falling down, so things can fall in place. You don't want to try to move faster than your pace. Life throws punches, so think of that fall as an even bigger blow you dodged. In the midst of falling, stay positive. That opportunity you fall into may be bigger than what you originally had planned for yourself.

☐195. "You're spending so much time with other people that you don't know who you are yourself."

We all want to be accepted to a certain extent, so that may cause us to bend a little. We like some people so much that we sacrifice the things we truly want just to be closer to them or around them. The problem with that is you don't get to know yourself. How much time do you spend alone? Find out what you like, or do something that you solely want to do. Can you go watch a movie by yourself? Can you find out what you like about yourself? We are all individuals with different brains, different skills, and different interests. Spend some time alone to find out who *you* really are.

☐196. "Be motivated by your struggle."

You didn't get to where you are in life by smooth sailing; you had to overcome some trouble. In order to get where you want to go, sometimes you have to take a mental trip back down memory lane to see how strong you have been in the past. Look at the obstacles you've faced in the past, especially the ones that seemed as though there was no way out of, but somehow, someway you persevered through. Let those situations inspire you to get through your current situations. They are confirmation that you can—and will—get through your current storms.

Discipline your grind

Week 29:

☐ **197.** *"Knowing* **what you have to do and** *doing* **what you have to do are two different things."**

Be honest with yourself, if you really knew *exactly* what it took to make your dream a reality, would you still pursue it? If you knew the amount of hours you had to put in, the sacrifices you had to make, or if you had to invest your last on a consistent basis, would you still go after your dream? Are you willing to follow a blueprint that says, "You can't afford to eat lunch this month, there's no partying for a year, and you must wake up every day at 4am?" The majority of us would like to know, but over half of us wouldn't follow through if we knew. Well, I'm sad to tell you, but there is no blueprint. There is no perfect plan to success. Success is a long journey, and it's full of left turns, right turns, U-turns, yields signs, rerouting, and not to mention, the weather conditions. What you thought was a short-term journey could turn into a year-long quest. The point is, you won't know. All you can do is just be ready to grind. The fact that you don't know what's going to happen should also excite you. It should create optimism and hope that you will achieve your goal. The actual achievement is based on you alone and nobody else.

☐ **198. "If the plan doesn't work, don't change the goal. Restructure the plan and don't look down, it's an impossible view."**

You might have worked hard on a plan for months, and to you it may be perfect. I'm sorry to break it to you, but it's not. Along the way, some unexpected errors, un-calculated risks, and devastating losses may occur, but that should not deter you. Get back to the drawing board and touch up on the mishaps. Your plan isn't a failure; you just weren't as sharp as you thought you were, and that's okay. What separates the dream catchers from the daydreamers is the fact that the ones who are willing to keep trying after consistently failing know that each failure is a learning lesson and a step closer to a yes.

☐199. "A majority of the time, you have to discipline yourself to do the things you hate on a consistent basis in order to get to the things you love."

In life, we want to have our cake and eat it, too. With your dreams, that can't be the case. You have to be willing to give, to sacrifice, and to separate yourself from some of the things you are used in order to get to where you want to go. A majority of the time, the things we hate doing are the things we *have* to do to get the change we want. A major key to success is creating the ability and the mindset to overcome the laziness and the contentment we all have at some point in our lives. Believe in yourself.

☐200. "Stop looking at things as what you *have* to do and look at them as what you *get* to do. Your privilege is someone else's dream."

You complain about your job, you complain about where you live, you complain about what you eat, you complain about who you associate with, and you complain about what you wear. I don't mean to be harsh, but shut up, seriously! Everything you whine, bleat, and fuss about, someone else is praying for those very things. Instead of complaining all of the time, do something to change those circumstances. Most of the time, we have the ability to change the situations we are in, but we are too lazy and would rather talk about what needs to be done than actually do what it takes to make the change.

☐ **201. "Find out whatever it is you want, and go after it as if your life depends on it because it does."**

When I say your life depends on it, I don't mean that going after your dreams could be life or death, literally. But if you don't go after your dreams with everything you have, you will not live the way you dream of living, and you will die not living the life you've always dreamed of having. So, go after your dreams with all you have, so you can live the life you have always imagined.

☐ **202. "Don't let discomfort make you uncomfortable; it is there to challenge you, to help you grow, and to push you past your comfort zone."**

When you think of a headache, it is very uncomfortable, but in actuality you can still function correctly. That's the same attitude you have to have towards life. There are situations in life that will pop up and make you uncomfortable, and in the process, you develop growth. In every uncomfortable situation you face, you can't turn around, take a break, or try to avoid it; you will never grow. The best way to experience growth is to go through the things that are bad, and what better way to experience them than firsthand. Get comfortable with being uncomfortable.

☐ **203. "Positive thoughts make way for positive outlooks. Start this day thinking about how great it will be."**

Perception is what we think things are based on some sort of evidence, but that doesn't make it true. That can allow us to believe the total opposite of the truth based on something we sense. Apply that mindset to your thinking. Even if things are going bad, continue believing that everything is okay. The way you think can actually change your reality. You are what you *believe* you see in the mirror, not what you *think* you see.

Better yourself

Week 30:

☐204. **"Plant little positive seeds and show acts of love and kindness; you may not see the impact while you are alive, but that's what you can leave behind for the rest to build on to make the world a better place."**

Many people really want to change the world, but the problem is that they are afraid to start because they don't believe they can make a big enough impact. We have to get out of that state of mind; you have to know your contribution is needed. What you have to offer does matter, and so do you. Don't ever think that the world is too big for you to leave your mark, or for you to make a change. Just think, if Martin Luther King, Jr, Malcolm X, Rosa Parks, and others thought that way, then society wouldn't be where it is today.

☐205. **"The sweetest revenge is not for one to aim for equal or more pain towards another, but for one to reach enormous success."**

We always want to get back at people by making them feel bad, inflicting pain, or by showboating. That is not the way to be the bigger person. Chase your success, and when you reach it, remain a humble person. It's not your responsibility to make others feel bad just because you reached success. If you don't show humility, you can hinder your chances for further growth and put your current success in jeopardy. It isn't worth the headache; revenge can be a never-ending circle. Don't engage in it.

☐206. **"You can only be the best you can be if you are honest with yourself."**

If you aren't true to who you say you are through your actions, you will never get to where you want to go. The only way to become the best you can be is to work on yourself at all times, especially when no one is looking. That is when you are being tested; if you can be true to yourself when no one is around to see what you do, you can achieve anything you want.

☐207. **"Stop creating ideas when you know you don't have the work ethic to follow through, you are fooling yourself. Either create a work ethic, or work for someone who has one."**

A lot of times, we think of ways to achieve financially, socially, and athletically inclined goals. But with those thoughts must come a dedicated work ethic. You must create the ability to exert extra energy to those added on pressures of your already busy life. You have to be real with yourself. If you think you have too much on your plate, focus on your current goals, and then slowly add another goal. Don't pile on more than you can take. Adding on a new challenge isn't supposed to be easy, but in the long run, it is usually worth it, and you *can* benefit from it.

☐208. **"You don't get to success just on talent alone; you have to dish out effort and sacrifice."**

Just because you are good at what you do, don't think that skillset alone will take you where you want to go. Talent can make you slightly above average, but what it takes to reach and maintain success is a consistent and hard work ethic.

Continuously practicing, studying, and working is a recipe for success.

□209. "You can go from barely making it to making more than enough. Now, it's time for you to start believing it and dishing out the work ethic."

It's easy to look at someone else and think, "How did they do that?" or, "How did they make it that far?" You're focusing on the wrong thing. You need to be asking them to show you, to teach you, to mentor you. Stop spending so much time questioning someone else's success. Either ask them for help, or put in the work to get to that same point and beyond. If you don't possess a work ethic or can't create one for yourself, get used to being average.

□210. "Keep people around you who love you enough to offend you. They only offend you with the intent to tell you the truth, not to tear you down and keep you there."

The first problem is that you are hanging out with people who are more worried about your feelings rather than your well-being. They say things to make you feel good instead of speaking truth. As long as they make you feel comfortable, you will never be able to better yourself because even if you are wrong in a situation, they will tell you that everything is okay when it's really not. You need to be confronted when you mess up and understand that your behavior is unacceptable. Next time, you *must* be better!

Release the strongholds

Week 31:

☐ **211. "Don't turn yesterday's feelings into today's problems. Today has its own trials, keep moving forward."**

You can't worry about spilled milk. Those problems from yesterday are the ones that you can't control. Let them go; they can cloud your thinking and cause unwanted stress. Each day will bring its own trials and tribulations, so there's no need to bring in any more. Worry about what's ahead of you because what's behind you is just that, behind you.

☐ **212. "Each trial you overcome is your own prerequisite to the next positive step in whatever you are in pursuit of."**

A trial is nothing but a bump along your journey. When it presents itself, it doesn't mean turn around. It means dig deep inside of yourself, and find the will to overcome adversity. Every time you overcome something negative, it is usually followed with some sort of positivity, even if the only positive thing is you overcoming your trials. Look at your trials as an opportunity to create happiness for yourself, and not as setback.

☐ **213. "What you feed yourself is the key to growth and success. Mind, body, and soul feed yourself the right things."**

You can't learn how to be successful until you learn what successful people have done. Study them. Listening to music that carries no substance or shows no value to where you want to go in life is wasted time. Music is a heavy influence on how you dress, talk, and act; choose what you listen to wisely. Everyone can't handle everything the same way. You can't let just anybody into your life, thinking they are good for you. They could just be there to corrupt you or lead you to make bad decisions. You have come a long way, so there is no need for distractions and roadblocks. Keep things in perspective.

☐214. "More sacrificing and less excuses. No blaming and work harder."

If you can't get motivated to get to where you want to be, hold yourself accountable. Put in more work than you usually would, but you can't complain and blame others. You don't deserve success if you aren't willing to put in the work. If you can't change yourself, you can't expect more change in your pocket, or your life.

☐215. "There's too much potential for success to sit back and complain about what you should be and could be doing."

You better invest in developing a good work ethic and take what's out there for you. Too often, we make excuses for where we are and we blame other people for our lack of success. Well, success starts with you and the type of effort you dish out. If you cheat yourself, your income will be short as well.

☐216. "At times in your journey towards success, you will have to fight your way through the pain, you will have to push through sickness, and you will have to push through the loss of loved ones. Push your way through!"

It's not about the size of the dog in the fight; it's about the size of the fight in the dog. Tough times will present themselves for as long as you live, and your job is to do whatever it takes to overcome those struggles, and then share your story with others to give them the motivation to do the same. Each adversity you face brings with it the potential to mature your growth. Everybody goes through things, just because they don't wear their feelings on their sleeves doesn't mean they aren't dealing with their own struggles.

☐ **217. "Don't give up, don't give in, get through it. That challenge challenged you because it thought it could conquer you, prove it wrong."**

The easiest thing in life is to give up and throw in the towel, but the true character of a person lies in how that person responds to adversity. You learn nothing from giving up, only that you are a quitter. In pushing through a struggle, you learn how much you can endure, how strong you are, and how tough your skin is. Challenges are to be accepted, not neglected. You got this!

Give 120%

Week 32:

☐ **218. "Go for the win and nothing else; however, if you do not win, be brave in the attempt. Have confidence!"**

Nobody likes to lose and people hate to tie. We all desire to win with everything in life. Just because you worked hard and have dedicated a lot of time does not guarantee a win, remember that. Whatever the outcome is, don't ever leave yourself wondering if you could have done more. Give 120%, so you can't question your effort in the end.

☐ **219. "Sometimes the right path isn't the easiest one, but either way you must stay strong."**

When in pursuit of your dreams, there will be plenty of forks in the road. One may be easy and smooth sailing—or at least you think it is—and the other may be hard from the start. You have to choose the best path for you, or what you think is the best path for you. No matter what road you choose, that does no exempt you from facing hard times. The key is staying strong and trusting your choices, knowing that in the long run everything will work out in your favor.

☐ **220. "You have to be able to look at nothing to see everything; that's called vision, and without that, you have no dream."**

Sometimes to find out what you love and what you love to do, you need to be alone to think. It may consist of staring at beautiful nothingness, somewhere or something that allows your mind to create a picture and a vision of what you want for your life. It's hard to create a vision with a cloudy mind full of life's problems and everyone else trying to tell you theirs. Go to a place of peace and meditate. The visions will come, and it's up to you to act on them.

☐221. "Do not let a nightmare keep you from your dreams."

A majority of the time we have a vision, and we even get as far as planning how we will achieve our vision, but the nightmare overshadows the good and the achievements we saw to begin with. With a fearful mindset, we will never take the first step and our dreams will merely be just that, a dream. Until you decide to chase your dream, you will continue to live in a nightmare.

☐222. "Don't compare yourself to the next person; there is always someone doing better than you, just as there is always someone doing worse."

Don't get caught up in comparing yourself to others. What always looks better isn't always better; it just *looks* that way. For all you know, those particular people may use materialistic things to overshadow the pain they really feel. What you do know is that you aren't doing as badly as you think you are, and there is someone else who is wishing and praying that they were in your shoes. Don't be so stubborn that you can't realize your current blessings; you can lose them being ungrateful.

☐223. "No matter how you see yourself, you are special. The mistakes you made in the past don't define you."

Everyone has made mistakes in the past and will continue to make mistakes in the future. However, the mistakes you make in the future should not be the same ones you made in the past. Your past mistakes should have taught you a lesson. Know that the past does not define you and each day you have a new slate, another chance. Use your opportunities wisely and show growth from your previous immaturity. Not only for society, but for yourself, as well. You are capable of being a better person.

☐ 224. "People don't live their lives based on what you tell them, they live it based on who you are."

It is so easy to hold a conversation and talk highly about yourself, but if you have no proof of action about the things you've claimed to do, people will pay you no mind. For example, I informed many people that I was writing a book and everyone was like, "Yeah, okay" or "Sure, whatever," but when my book was published, all I heard was, "You wrote a book?" or "I didn't think you were serious!" People will not take you seriously until you decide to take yourself seriously. So, when you say you are going to do something, make sure you stick to it or keep your mouth closed.

Dreaming is cool...pursuing is better

Week 33:

☐225. **"It will all be worth it when you conquer your own world in due time."**

On the road to your dreams, you may feel like it's just a never-ending journey. You have been grinding for 6 months, 1 year, 5 years, or maybe even longer, and that's okay because you are *still* grinding. Do not get discouraged; this race is not won by the swift, but by the one willing to endure. If nothing has put a permanent stop to your chase, there is still a chance of catching and living your dream. Don't let the amount of time you've already put into the dream take away the joy and excitement of the pursuit.

☐226. **"Pursuit of happiness is just that, a journey. The choice is up to you."**

On the Declaration of Independence, it says we have been given the right to pursue happiness. It never said that actual happiness would be given to us, just that we had the right to *pursue* it. Continue to work hard in your pursuit of happiness, the road will get bumpy and you may fail a couple of times, but don't let that deter you. Usually when you feel like giving up, that's when you are arriving at your breakthrough. Be strong!

☐227. **"You can't be a dreamer all your life. Eventually, you have to wake up and chase one of them. Or you will sleepwalk through life."**

Everyone has a dream, but not everyone is bold enough chase that dream. People have their reasons, whether it's because they are scared of success, scared of being defeated, scared of what others will think, or wonder if they will be accepted. All of that is irrelevant; all that matters is whether or not your dream will create happiness for you. Either pursue your dreams, or work for somebody else and live in a nightmare.

☐228. "Preparation and destiny can coexist. If you work hard enough, you just might get lucky and come across the opportunity needed to become successful."

You may think things just happen, but that's never really the case. In some form, you have done something to gain the opportunity; otherwise, it wouldn't have presented itself. I'm not saying that you will get rewarded for every good thing you do, but I *am* saying that if you focus on the grind, focus on the preparation, and focus on working hard, it's only right that you benefit. The universe takes you seriously and does you a favor. Never want handouts, always work for it.

☐229. "You might think it's your destiny, but don't get that confused with your destination."

In life, we often start out headed one way and it seems like the right path, only to later find out that it was just a short-lived moment. It is *then* that our lives begin to head in another direction. Don't be afraid of this change because that previous journey was growth to prepare you for what's next to come, and the new direction you are now headed.

☐230. "The only way in life to be number one in anything is to be different."

It's very simple; in order to reach that competitive greatness, you have to set yourself apart, you have to work differently and think differently. That requires you to put in more than the standard number of hours other people are putting in. To reach your dream, you need tunnel vision. Having this mindset is what sets you apart; it's what makes you different. You have to be willing to step outside of the box and be different in order to do what others *aren't* doing.

☐231. "Until you decide to chase your dream, you will continue to live in a nightmare."

If you don't chase your dream, you've allowed your fate to be put in someone else's hands. They tell you when to come to work, how much they want to pay you, what you have to do, and this is all because you work for them. It's all because you *need* to work for them. Until you tell the universe what you want by speaking it into existence and actually pursuing it, you will never be satisfied. At least in the quest for your dreams, you know that the outcome of your life will be based on your decisions, and not the ones other people have made for you.

Take the bad with the good

Week 34:

☐232. **"Be thankful for it all the highs, the lows, the blessings, the lessons, the setbacks, the love, and the hate."**

In life, we tend to only show thanks for the positive things that we go through, which is normal. But start to show gratitude for the trials that you get to face and are allowed to overcome; some people have faced the same exact challenges, only they weren't successful at all. Show thanks for everything you go through; we aren't promised anything.

☐233. **"Know the difference between failing and being a failure."**

Even though you have experienced defeat, you *must* understand that there is a difference between failure and failing. If you don't get the results you want, that's okay. It doesn't make you a failure. Don't confuse who you are with what you dish out. For example, Michael Jordan, Serena Williams, Steve Jobs, and others have tasted defeat on numerous occasions, but are they failures? No! Do whatever you can, with where you are in life, and with what you have. Don't ever accept defeat and never be satisfied or content.

☐234. **"Today, don't let the world dictate your aspirations as a human being. You are capable of achieving anything."**

The world can be a very tough place; it can tear you down mentally, physically, and emotionally if you let it. Only you can decide if you want to better your life, nobody else can do that for you. People will say things to make you feel bad and try to tell everything you *can't* do. That's not true unless you listen to it and believe it. Sometimes, you have to be your own motivation, your own reason for why you want to accomplish certain goals. Wake up every day, knowing that you can achieve anything you put your heart and your mind to.

☐ **235. "Slow and correct is better than quick and inaccurate."**

We as a society have gotten used to everything coming to us at a fast pace. Fast-food restaurants, microwavable food, and 4G networks. With these quick, fast, and in a hurry everyday necessities, we have created an impatient mindset because we are so used to everything being delivered so instantly. I'm sorry to break it to you, but your dreams won't happen that instantly. If anything, that's the *one* thing that will take patience and time. It may take months or years for you to make your dream a reality. Anything that comes fast, either isn't good for you, or it won't last long.

☐ **236. "Your determination determines your destination."**

Your happiness cannot depend on anybody else, in no way, shape, or form. The day you depend on someone else to put a smile on your face is the day you don't value your worth. If no one has yet told you, you are capable of creating self-happiness. Whatever you want, chase it; whatever you think, believe it; and whatever you want to do, achieve it!

☐ **237. "Don't confuse rest with laziness; if you aren't where you want to be in life, then you need to rest less,**

get rid of the laziness, and do more work. You *have* to know somebody chasing your spot."

Everyone gets tired and believes he or she needs a break or rest, and in some cases that may be true. Ask yourself this question, "Is my rest worth more than my success?" If not, you should feel uncomfortable resting so much. You shouldn't even want to rest when you are in pursuit of your dreams. Your dreams should make you upset that you have to go to sleep for a short period of time, but make you excited to wake up and get back to work.

☐**238. "One of the most misinterpreted sayings is, 'Practice makes perfect'."**

Everyone likes to assume that this quote is saying that good practice makes perfect, and if you perfect something, it's permanent. But if you look at the actual quote, it doesn't specify what kind of practice you are in engaging in. The way the quote is worded, you *can* practice bad habits and perfect the wrong thing. The key thing to remember is that good practice is what you need to upgrade your craft. At times, it may get overwhelming because you may not see the growth right away. But when it's time to perform, you and others will notice the difference. All of your hard work will not be in vain; you must believe that! The value of the reward comes from the appreciation you show for what you do through your dedicated work ethic.

Forward progress

Week 35:

☐ **239. "Baby steps can take you a ways over time. At the end of the day, it's all about forward movement. That's what really matters."**

Don't get discouraged if the only steps you seem to be making now are baby steps, that's okay, as long you are moving forward is what *really* matters. We tend to get upset at how slow our progression is taking, and that may be due to the other people around us moving faster, or it could just be that you are being impatient. Whatever the case may be, you have to show patience; as long as your progress continues to be forward, you are moving at your correct speed. Be quick, but don't hurry, and by that I mean, do what you can as fast, as accurate, and as perfect as possible. Don't try to speed up what you have no control over.

☐ **240. "So many people have written you off, but that's neither here nor there. Have you written yourself off is the real question."**

People will have their doubts, talk their trash, and look at you sideways, but so what? Don't let that affect you. You cannot control how others think or feel about you, but you *can* control how you think and feel about yourself. Don't count yourself out of any battle before you even go to war. Those battles aren't always what they seem, but you will never know if you don't fight.

☐241. **"Success doesn't have an alarm clock or a bedtime."**

You can't get caught up in trying to get a certain amount of sleep. In pursuit of success, you won't be able to get that normal 6 to 8 hours in. Some days you may only get 5 or 6 hours of sleep. You have to know that what seems to be unrewarded, will now be rewarded over time in the future. A majority of today's successful business owners do not get 7 hours of sleep, and they are millionaires. What makes you think you deserve 8 hours?

☐242. **"A basic mindset can't get you to extraordinary measures."**

Don't ever be under the impression that any goal is too big. You have to be able to see yourself achieving big before you get there. In thinking big, you must possess or create an even bigger work ethic. Don't get intimidated or distracted by anything; remain focused on your vision, and go above and beyond to make it reality.

☐243. **"Life is about resiliency, being able to bounce back. Do not aim to *not* fail because setbacks are inevitable in the pursuit of your dreams. Aim to be successful by any means."**

Everyone has a plan until life throws storms their way, and then they want to run back to the safety net. You have to realize that no matter what you do, life is going to throw some counter punches to your actions; you can't let that scare you. You must learn to bounce back stronger, and stay positive through it all, no matter what. The moment you start thinking negatively is when you allow yourself to believe it. Continue to pursue your dreams and block as many of life's punches as you can, but never throw in the towel. Every round is important! Remember, you aren't promised tomorrow, so go hard today.

☐244. "Sometimes, in order find out who you really are, you have to get away from everything you know."

The saying, "Be quiet, I can't hear myself think," is a prime example here. You are around so many people, so many visions, and so many influences that you don't know what you really like or who you really are. People do their best to persuade others to like what they like; that's why there are so many followers in the world. It's not too often that you hear about a one-man bank robbery; time was spent persuading others to join in, regardless of how bad they *didn't* want to participate. Try getting away from your influences, your social networks, your family and friends, and whatever else it takes to create some alone time with yourself. Go some place where you can think clearly and find out what you like and what you really want to do.

☐245. "Are you in love with your dream? Or are you in love with what it may bring?"

What's your purpose? Are you doing it because you love it, or because of what it might bring? Let's say you do it because of what it brings, and you get everything you wanted out of it. Now what? You may get bored and make dumb decisions because your high is crashing. You no longer have the drive because you now have what you have always desired. However, if you do it for the love, you can reap all of your desires and more, and your drive will always be there because you did it for the love and not for the benefits.

Keep your distance from mediocrity

Week 36:

☐246. **"Be comfortable doing what you want to do; don't wait for someone else to do it, or for someone to give you confirmation that it's okay to do what you want."**

Be okay with your decisions, you don't need anyone's approval to go after whatever you want. Don't worry about what people think or say because regardless of the outcome, there will still be negative and positive opinions about what you do or have done. Don't let that stop you! You should be your own biggest critic and your biggest supporter. You got this, now go for it!

☐247. **"Rise and grind, or sleep and struggle."**

There aren't too many people who really like to wake up in the morning. But if you think about it, after you take care of your hygiene, the morning is when you have the most energy. Nothing comes from sleep but dreams and nightmares. Eventually, you have to wake up and chase that dream, or continue to live in a nightmare. You will feel so much better after you get up and put some work in.

☐248. **"Time management is always about how you prioritize your life. It's about what's more important to you."**

People always say, "I have to manage my time better." No, you just have to have your priorities together. You know everything that needs to be done, and you also know what you want to do. The problem is your wants outweigh your needs. In the pursuit of your dreams, that won't be a productive recipe; you need to reprioritize and sustain some discipline. Don't act faithful to your grind for a week, and then go back to your old ways and wonder why nothing is changing. You are too inconsistent to see change. Be real with yourself!

☐249. "It's better to be alone than surrounded by bad company."

You can focus if you are by yourself and have no negativity surrounding you. You may become lonely, but to become number one in anything you have to be different. Why be surrounded by unmotivated, unambitious, and undriven people who will eventually bring you down and stop your growth? There is nothing wrong with grinding alone because at the end of the day, you aren't trying to share your paycheck.

☐250. "The reason you aren't successful is because what you advertise and who you really are doesn't add up."

First of all, quit lying to yourself. Things aren't working out for you because you are promoting a false air about yourself. When you start being honest about who you really are, through your work ethic and attitude, you will see some major changes and some positive results. Until then, you will keep disappointing yourself. I'm not saying this to be mean, I'm saying this to be real. You can't sugarcoat every lesson in life. You have to take some harsh criticism to be successful in life.

☐251. **"Don't let your ego become bigger than your dream. Just as quickly as you achieved success, you can lose it even faster. Humility!"**

Don't think you are all that and more, acting like you are bigger than the grind, bigger than the dream, or bigger than people who supported you. Yes, you put in the work, the hours, and the money, but that doesn't give you the right to treat people differently, or to act in a different way towards people. Be humble, or watch people enjoy your downfall more than they enjoy your come up.

☐252. **"Your dreams are reachable and obtainable."**

Your dreams aren't bigger than you, don't ever think that! However, they may be bigger than your work ethic, so don't get the two mixed up. You are capable of achieving and reaching all of your heart's desires, but if you don't possess or develop the necessary work ethic and drive, it will stay a dream and never become an achievement. Think big, work harder.

Can't shine without the grind

Week 37:

☐ **253. "In order to reach that dream life, you have to put in that dream work."**

Many people want a healthy and financially stable life, but if you aren't putting in the necessary hours, then you won't get that dream life. Luck is for leprechauns, and last I checked, we humans aren't green. You have to go through the necessary struggle—the grind—and persevere through it all. It won't be easy, but it will be well worth it to live the life you have always imagined for yourself.

☐ **254. "Everyone has a dream, but the grind doesn't come with it."**

Don't get it twisted, dreams come a dime a dozen. One thing for certain is that the hustle needed is sold separately. Everyone has a dream, but most don't try to pursue their dream when they find out just how much time and effort is required to make it work. As much as you want that dream, you have to be willing to grind even harder.

☐ **255. "If you only work on your dreams the days you feel like it, they will forever be dreams and never achievements."**

Without any added activities, our lives are already busy. Our days consist of working 8 hours a day, working out before or after work, cooking dinner, and get ready for the next day. In between that, you find time to socialize and hang out. Also, if you are pursuing a dream—whether it's writing a book, starting a company, or taking classes—it can all be overwhelming. However, that dream you are pursuing needs to be pursued daily, meaning you can't take any days off. Of course, there will be some days that unexpected things come up and you can't always make time for your dream, but you have to set aside consistent hours that you will put into the dream. If you keep getting to it when it's convenient, you will never achieve it. Discipline is needed to make it a reality.

☐ **256. "To be successful, you don't need the approval of anyone. You just need a tremendous work ethic. That's the biggest known secret."**

The reason it's the biggest known secret is because people have no problem telling you how they became successful. They know if you won't put in the work—whether it's because you are afraid to fail, you feel you can't handle success, or you're just full of excuses—you will prevent yourself from reaching success. Those feelings will get you nowhere; they will only leave you feeling sorry for yourself.

☐ **257. "The difference between who you are and who you want to become is what you are doing in between that time."**

We all want to be great and do great things, but our words, our actions, and our relationships show differently. You have achievements you want to reach and you see yourself reaching them, but ask yourself if what you are doing now is the correct way to get there. You know what you should and should not be doing, and who you should or should not be hanging out with. It's on you to sacrifice for your dreams. Nobody is going to come to you and say, "I'm going to stop hanging around you because I'm keeping you from your dream." No! That's on you to make that decision.

☐ **258. "The depth of your earning will come from the depth of your learning."**

Learn as much as you can because that is the one thing no one can take from you. If you work your situations correctly, you can talk your way into a *great* situation. Never forget that knowledge alone isn't power, but *applied* knowledge is. You can know everything in the world, but if you don't apply it to your life correctly, it's pointless to have the knowledge to begin with. So, learn all you can, apply all you know, and watch what comes your way.

☐ **259. "What you are going through is not the end, it's just a moment."**

In life, it always seems like the greatest of times are short-lived and the toughest of times are never-ending. You have to learn to take the good with the bad, just know that the rain won't last forever, and soon the sun will shine again. In addition, surround yourself with supportive individuals who will help you through the tough times. The supportive people are the ones who are around during the good *and* the bad moments in your life.

How is your mindset?

Week 38:

☐ **260. "No matter what you think, you are doing better than good and better than most."**

Don't compare yourself to others because there is *always* someone doing better than you, and there is *always* someone doing worse than you. The only person you should compare yourself to is you. Compare yourself today to who you were yesterday and see if you have made any progress. Keep your eyes focused on your growth and no one else.

☐ **261. "When you are working on something that you want to achieve, you have got to sell yourself on that vision every day."**

The more you increase your belief in your vision, the more possibility it has to become a reality. If you can't believe in your own vision every day and see it as a success, how can you expect someone else to? Don't let anyone downplay your vision; you know what you see. If you believe it can work, hold on to it and take the necessary steps to make it a reality.

☐ **262. "Going through failure to achieve your goals takes courage, but it is also a needed experience."**

Many people can't accept rejection, failure, or the word "no". It is a tough thing to swallow, especially if you put your all into something and you fail. But the thing about the word "no" is that it's only permanent if you accept it. You have the ability to keep trying until you get a "yes". The decision to pursue a "yes" is on you. You have to be willing to endure.

☐263. **"Knowledge is wealth, you can't get to where you want to go and not educate yourself on what you are trying to do."**

The first step to pursuing a dream is having a vision of how to achieve it. The second is educating yourself on how to do it the proper way. A lot of people fail because they aren't educated on what they want to do. That is like having a test that you haven't even studied for, yet you still expect an A. That won't happen! You have to educate yourself, but just because you educate yourself does not exclude you from making mistakes. However, you will make a lot more mistakes if you remain uneducated about your dream.

☐264. **"This thing we call life promises you one thing, and that's that you will not get out alive."**

To many, that is a scary statement. However, let that drive you to accomplish everything that you can while you are still alive. You have the ability to achieve, pursue, or try anything you want to on this earth, so do it while you can. When you leave this earth, you don't want to take any unused talents and ideas with you to the grave. Who does *that* benefit? No one.

☐265. **"Your yesterdays don't matter, don't convict yourself today for yesterday's failures."**

The past *can* have an impact on your future, but it can't determine it. So, don't get caught up on what you did or didn't do. From today on, you have the power to make the rest of your life the best of your life. Move forward and think ahead.

☐266. "Hold on to your vision. Stop worrying about how you are going to get there. You have to continuously prepare yourself for what you want because you expect to get it."

What you are chasing is out there and it's obtainable to you, you just have to believe it. You can't get caught up on how far you think you are from reaching the goal. You have to realize the more work you put in towards it, the closer you are getting to it. The only thing that is between you and your destination is you and what you are *not* doing.

You have to push through!

Week 39:

☐267. **"If you do your best and that's still not enough, then you have to do more than what is required."**

We usually underestimate how much we are able to endure; you will never know how strong you really are until you are placed in certain situations where being strong is the only option you have. Keep knocking on the door; no one can ignore your knocks forever. Eventually, someone will open the door. However, if that door does not open, you will have to knock down the wall.

☐268. **"Don't become a potential-never-realized person, don't become a has-dreams-that-were-never-pursued person, or a never-used-my-gifts-and-talents person."**

What are you saving your talents, your gifts, and your potential for? You are here to share it with others, and along the way, you can gain wealth, achievement, and knowledge. Pursue anything and everything you have ever wanted to, max out your potential, and use *all* of your gifts. Don't be selfish and keep your blessings to yourself.

☐269. **"Irresponsible people will never tell you they are irresponsible, and because they are irresponsible, you can't rely on them to make your dreams come true."**

You are responsible for yourself, so if you aren't happy with where you are, it's up to you to change it. Your happiness and your success are in your hands; you have the ability to climb every mountain and overcome any obstacle. You can't rely on others to do anything for you; they will either let you down or stand you up. If they do help out, that will only make you dependent on others. Learn to do for yourself.

☐270. "Every fall down ain't a downfall."

You have to learn how to see the good in every situation, no matter how bad it looks. What you think is a setback could be a setup for a comeback, but you have to *look* at it that way. Everything you lose isn't really a loss, remember that.

☐271. "Honestly, if you can't be used, you are useless."

Being used is not always a bad thing, for instance, if someone calls you and says, "I need you to create a web page," that's an opportunity for you. Don't always look at it as, "They only call when they need something." Yes, you are being used, but you are *positively* being used. Someone is telling you that they value your gifts and your talents. Your gifts and your talents allow you to create opportunities for yourself, they allow you to make a name for yourself, and they allow you to make some money out of it as well. Learn the difference between being useful and being useless. Believe it or not, people will always see you as one or the other.

☐272. "If you want to see a difference, be a difference."

Everyone talks about how the community, the country, and the world needs change, but what are you contributing to help the change start? There is more to it than just posting messages on social networks; it requires hands-on work. Start a nonprofit to help the youth, feed the homeless, or physically help clean the environment. Actually, you don't even have to start an organization, just join one! If everyone who makes the statement, "The world needs a change,"

EARL JACKSON

contributes, we would see a *big* difference. Let it start with you.

☐273. **"Until you start to take yourself seriously, stop getting mad at people for taking you as a joke."**

If you don't respect yourself, what makes you think others will? When I say "respect", I mean the way you walk, talk, dress, and think. You have to carry yourself the way you want to be treated. You are not at joke or a game, so stop playing yourself and develop some meaningful values to live by.

Move different

Week 40:

☐ **274. "Only the people who are not doing what they love hate going to work."**

The only way to survive in this world is to work. The thing about work is you have to do something that you love, so you will never feel like you are "working". Many people settle for jobs they really hate just to survive. In reality, you have a choice. I suggest you look for something that you love doing, make a career out of it, and never hate your job again.

☐ **275. "Is your rest worth more than your success?"**

Yes, the body needs hours to recuperate from life, but are you oversleeping? Have you ever noticed that if you don't sleep enough, you are tired, and if you sleep too long, you are also tired? Your mind can play tricks on you, so you have to train it to chase success. After making it a habit to sacrifice some of your rest, your brain will pick up the pattern, and what once seemed like hell will soon become a habit. That is when you have created a new normal for yourself.

☐ **276. "You think you deserve more? Work harder."**

We all believe that we deserve more, but ask yourself, "Have I put in the work?" You can't expect to get rewarded for something you didn't do. That's like getting MVP for your team, and you sat on the bench! We have to stop thinking that we are entitled to receive more when that's not even the case. You get what you work for, so if you want more, then do more. Stop crying and start grinding.

☐277. **"You have to aim for something. If you aim for nothing, that's just what you will get, nothing. Set goals so that you have something to chase."**

Some people just live life, looking forward to nothing but the next day. You need to have a 5-year, a 10-year, or 15-year plan. Work towards something in life, whether it's a degree or starting a business, but whatever it is, chase it! If you have nothing to pursue, you are content with your life and that means you will be comfortable with the same job, the same pay, the same car, and the same home forever. Never let contentment set in.

☐278. **"Sleep and starve, or rise and grind."**

The only thing you can conquer while sleeping is sleep, and that's not an accomplishment to be proud of. For instance, you had a day off and someone asks you what you did. Your response is, "Sleep!" You mean to tell me, you did nothing all day? If you don't know, there's no such thing as catching up on sleep, and you won't be able to get those hours back, either. You might as well be productive with your free time and stop trying to get in quick naps. Sleeping will only allow you to dream your dream, not accomplish it. Get up and grind!

☐279. **"Be disciplined with your dreams, be consistent in chasing them, and be humble when achieving them."**

There will be days where you are mentally, physically, and emotionally exhausted, but those are the best days to put in the work because you will feel even better afterwards. Discipline yourself to attack those days you don't want to grind. Be consistent in your grind. Know that your grind isn't going unnoticed, or that it isn't being unappreciated. When you do reach the mountain top, act as if you knew this was going to happen because you did, otherwise you wouldn't have chased it!

☐280. "Your preference won't get you to your purpose."

If you want to get to a certain place in life, but you are not willing to give up on certain things, you have a very unsuccessful plan, and it won't work. If you want a better body, but you don't prefer waking up early to run, that's another unsuccessful plan. You can't want change when you aren't willing to do the work. That unwillingness will be the main reason why you don't succeed. You have to get out of your own way.

Self-Evaluation

Week 41:

☐ **281.** **"You have built your life, regardless of whether or not you like where you are. However, if you don't like who you are, what you have, or your relationships, it's up to you to tear it all down and rebuild your dream life."**

The good thing about a bad moment is that it is only temporary; you have the power to make your life the way you want it, but it will take an effort that you probably aren't used to. If you want to change the things that are going on with you, you can—just know it may be one of the hardest things you will ever have to do. You have to discipline yourself to get away from the habits you have had for years, and you must space yourself from individuals you have known for years with a sense of urgency to make a change quickly, knowing that time is not on your side.

☐ **282.** **"Take 100% responsibility for your effort, your life, your opportunities, and your happiness."**

You have to hold yourself accountable for everything that goes on in your life. You can't blame other people for your lack of happiness, your lack of success, or any other inconsistencies in your life. You have the power to change *everything* in your life. So, until you take on the full responsibility of making your life what you want it to be, don't get upset with any one else but yourself. Don't like it? Change it!

☐283. "Every obstacle has the potential to be an opportunity."

Too often, we look at the obstacles life throws us as trials and tribulations instead of as favorable times and chances. Those obstacles we tend to look at as negative also present us with the chance to be extraordinary. Everything is based on how you perceive it and how you process the situation. If you believe it to be a trial, that's what it will be. If you go in believing that it is an opportunity, then that's what it will be. However you see it, that's on you. Change the way you think!

☐284. "You might have to go down before you can go up."

One day, I was in a parking garage with a friend, and we were trying to find the exit, but the exit sign was only sending us *further* underground. We were going downwards for about three minutes, and after a while, we thought about turning around because continuing to go down made no sense. My friend said, "Let's turn around," and just before we turned around, we saw a light that led us to the street. It was awkward to experience an exit like that. We thought we were heading the wrong way, when the whole time we were on the right path. Talk about not believing! I'm sharing this story to demonstrate that your dreams might take you on a path that you are sure is the wrong way, but it's not. Just follow the directions a little while longer, and it will eventually give you signs that it is indeed the correct path.

☐285. "Don't let everything around you change while you stay the same."

Every day the world is changing and evolving; something new is being invented every second. You have to move, evolve, and change with the times. Nobody is responsible for you but you; you are lucky to have an alarm clock to help you get up. That's about the only thing you should expect out of life. Life is about change, and the people who don't change as life progresses are stuck on their last move, going nowhere fast. You better get to moving, the world won't stop for you, so don't stop for nothing.

☐286. "Stop asking what's wrong with it and ask what's right about it."

We all do things in life and see no problem with doing them; they aren't illegal and we aren't harming anyone. However, how is that helping *you*? With the time that you spend on the activities that have no real purpose, you could be using that time to do something very constructive instead. For example, working on your dreams and your goals, or giving back to the community are constructive activities. Do something that has meaningful value, don't participate in something meaningless that *you* gave value.

☐287. "Act like you've been in the moment before."

When you *do* reach your goals, don't act like you aren't used to the outcome. You set out to achieve a goal, so you had to be expecting to reach it. You knew that the moment was going to happen eventually, you just didn't know *when*. There's no need to act like you never knew because you knew all along. To sum it up, be humble, have humility, and be modest; it will take you beyond what you dreamed of. Nobody likes a prideful person.

Well-Rounded

Week 42:

☐ 288. "Don't just be inspired, be inspiring."

It's not very hard to be inspired; there are hundreds of videos, thousands of books, and plenty of speakers. But the real task after you get your fuel is, can you pour that same fuel into someone else who is lacking the motivation? At one point in time, you were in their shoes and someone else motivated you! So, take on the challenge of motivating someone else. Be the person who inspires someone else. If you think you have no story, think about the toughest time in your life and how someone else helped you through it.

☐ 289. "You learn more from failure and adversity than you learn from success."

In every situation, you learn something, but you get more out of the situations you failed in and faced adversity than you get out of the situations that brought you success. With success, you might have only stuck by *some* of your values, but because the overall outcome was a success, you don't critique yourself as harshly as you would've if you experienced failure. When you fail, you go back to every situation, every plan, and you examine how you can better your overall approach, so that the next time you can achieve success.

☐ 290. "Don't embrace the thoughts that it won't happen, or that it can't happen. As soon as you say or think that, you've made that real."

If you don't believe your dreams and your goals are obtainable, how can you expect others to? You have to protect what you are chasing because people will try to shoot you down. Just because they aren't in the position to chase what they want, they will try to make you feel bad or guilty for just the thought of *wanting* a dream. Don't ever think that your dream is impossible because it is at that moment when you doubt yourself and your capabilities that you start to believe that the pursuit is impossible. In your pursuit, you don't need or want negative thoughts floating around in your head.

☐ **291. "You can't substitute excuses for hard work and expect to succeed."**

The easiest thing to come by in the pursuit of your dreams is an excuse. You can make an excuse for everything you don't accomplish, but in the end where will that get you? No one cares about the excuses you are making that prolong your dreams because they don't reap the benefits—or lose out—based on your productivity. This is *your* dream; you can't keep making excuses. It all comes down to either you are going to do it, or you aren't going to, it's that simple.

☐ **292. "Perseverance is the hard work you do *after* the hard work you already did."**

Many people possess a work ethic, but to possess perseverance in the face of adversity is a whole different ballgame. With perseverance, you find a reason to keep going, even when you have a hundred reasons to quit. Perseverance is usually needed after you have given all of the effort you thought you could possibly give. It requires you to dig deeper inside yourself and to find that extra effort you never knew you had. We all have that effort, but are you willing to stretch yourself to tap into it?

☐ **293. "When you *do* decide to chase your dream, you need to create a foundation for how you will get there."**

Once you get over the fear of deciding to chase your dream, now comes some of the real work. With your decision, you decided to do everything it takes to make your vision a reality, but it all starts with a plan, a blueprint. You have to take into account every precaution when building your foundation, while understanding that you can't plan for *every* single thing. Your plan is the most critical and maybe the most difficult part of your pursuit because it's the beginning. Don't get discouraged by the process; get excited because you know this is how you are going to achieve your goal.

☐ **294. "No matter how good of a person you are, there will always be someone criticizing you. You can't please everybody."**

The biggest mistake you can make in life is trying to please everyone. In doing so, you put yourself second or third, and trust me, your life is yours and *only* yours. If you don't put yourself first, no one else will. The word "loyalty" is misused these days. Everybody is loyal to someone or something, except themselves. Loyalty is showing faithfulness and obedience at all times. The only person you need to be loyal to is yourself because you know that whatever you chose to do, you are going to do it wholeheartedly with no doubt in mind. With that being said, put yourself first, and everyone else comes next.

Why not fail?

Week 43:

☐ **295. "Acknowledging your failures and taking criticism from others are two big steps to success."**

We all hate to fail and have someone tell us why we failed, and it's not just *what* they say, but *how* they say it. Some people hate it so much that they just give up; they don't even attempt to try again. Nothing comes from giving up, you just make it known that you were never really up for the challenge, and you don't want your dream as badly as you said you did. See, your mouth and your work ethic have to be equivalent to produce what you want. Accept the criticism. Don't worry about how it's presented to you, be glad that someone refuses to let you think that all is okay. Not every harsh statement should be taken personally.

☐ **296. "Failure can work to your advantage, if you put that block of failure down and use it as a stepping stone."**

The positive that comes from failing is that you are able to learn from the mistakes you made. You may fail more than two or three times, but make sure after each disappointment you learn something. Never come out of the situations you went through not learning anything and finding yourself making the same mistakes over and over again. Learn from your failures, and get back to work!

☐ **297. "Failure is only permanent when you give up. Don't give up, be resilient, and persevere through."**

We all have faced failure, but it's not permanent until you decide not to try anymore. Every "no" gets you a little closer to the "yes" you are searching for, just stay true to what you want to accomplish. Restructure the plan after each "no", and soon enough, you will reach your success. You must develop a mental toughness because hearing that your plan is wrong or hearing the word "no" time and time again can be overwhelming, but know that it's not the end. Keep pushing!

☐ 298. **"The reward will be much sweeter when you overcome failures than it is when you achieve and don't fail at all."**

The perseverance and mental toughness needed to overcome failure allows you to appreciate your dreams that much more than you would have if you hadn't failed at all. Of course, nobody wants to fail, but failure won't kill you. Failure only makes you stronger and more resilient, so don't get down on yourself if failure hits you. Shake it off and work harder; it's not the end of the world.

☐ 299. **"Let failure create an opportunity to be great, and don't let greatness put the fear of failure in your spirit."**

Some people expect you to fail, and that's fine. Where people mess up is when they don't expect you to keep going; that's where your greatness comes into play. It takes a lot for a person to keep hearing the word "no" and to keeping working towards their goal, anyway. People often give up after a while, but why? If you give up on yourself, how can you expect anyone else to believe in you? Greatness is obtainable by each and every one of us, but what are you willing to overcome to achieve it? How many "no's" can you take? How many failures can you persevere through?

☐300. **"You will find new limitations for yourself if you are willing to go harder than you did yesterday and today."**

Each day, push past the limit you set for yourself the day before. In doing that, you will find yourself at a new level in many aspects in your life. You may even find out that you have no limitations on how much you can achieve, on how successful you can be, or on how much you can inspire someone else. The harder you work, the more opportunities you create for yourself. Keep working; people are starting to notice.

☐301. **"If you are making it your business to be the best, then there is nothing more important than putting in the work to get better."**

If you continuously speak on being the best at anything, your main priority should be dedicating all of your idle time to being the best. You should be studying, practicing, and putting in the overtime. Hanging out should not be on your schedule, down time shouldn't exist, and your 8 to 10 hours of sleep should become 5 to 7 hours of rest. If you want to be great, you have to do what the greats do. There aren't many people born great, but they all work towards it. This is what some people refer to as, "insanity", and that is when you only engage in activities that will lead you to greatness. You can be great, but are you willing to sacrifice for greatness?

Effort doesn't go unnoticed

Week 44:

☐302. **"There is only one way to change yourself, and that's to challenge yourself. Create new limitations."**

The challenge of change only becomes hard when you aren't ready for change. When you decide to change, you test yourself to do the things you dislike to get to the things you want. You make change a habit, so your change can be permanent, and not just in the moment. Nobody said it would be easy, but it *will* be worth it.

☐303. **"There is no such thing as a second chance for a first impression, that means you have to be sharp every time you step out."**

Someone is always watching, and you are one judgment away from everything you have ever dreamed of. You are also one judgment away from everything you are not. You have to always be on point and always be professional. You never know who you might end up talking to, or who can help you. Opportunities come in different forms; it can be as simple as waiting in line to pay for food and sparking up a conversation with a stranger, unaware of the fact that this person could help you get a job or might be willing to invest in your vision. The world is both big and small at the same time.

☐304. **"Anything is possible, only if you are willing to do anything and everything to make it possible."**

All is possible unless you tell yourself otherwise, or allow others to influence you otherwise. You have to be willing to do everything possible to make your dream possible. It's as simple as refusing to accept the word "no". It's easier said than done, but it *can* be done.

☐305. **"Just because you had an off day doesn't mean you can take the day off. Where you are trying to go, days off are unacceptable."**

If you have a dream, you should be chasing it full blast. You don't have time for days off. There's no such thing as a day off to a dream chaser. They look forward to the off days, so they can spend the whole day focused on their dream. As of today, if you are chasing a dream, your last off day was your last day off.

☐306. **"Earn your expectations. If you expect greatness, dish out what it takes to get there. Only earn more, nothing less."**

You expect more money, you want a promotion, a new car, or a new house, but what are doing to achieve it? If you dish out mediocre effort, don't be upset with what you get back. Always dish out more with your work ethic than you expect to get in return, so you won't be disappointed with your reward at the end. If you want great, put in beyond great work ethic and you might achieve it.

☐307. **"Just because it looks improbable doesn't mean it's impossible."**

The word "impossible" should not exist in your vocabulary because nothing is impossible. You have to know at one point in time the things we do on a daily basis today were once thought of as impossible, like a cell phone, for example. How can we possibly be able to use a cell phone from anywhere, to use the internet, to pay bills, to listen to music, or to check the weather? If you think about it, that's amazing! Until Martin Cooper thought otherwise, cell phones were once considered part of the impossible. Whatever you want to create or achieve may have levels of difficulty to it, but it's not impossible.

☐308. **"Don't get discouraged from putting in the overtime when no one is watching because when it's time to perform, they will be able to recognize instantly that you stayed later without you saying one word."**

Just because no one is watching does not give you a reason to not put in the work before or after hours. *You* are watching yourself, and you can't cheat yourself, either. When you put in the work, opportunities will present themselves. But if you are never prepared, you can't get mad if nothing comes your way, and even if it does, you clearly aren't ready for it. You might put in the required time to do a job, but you need to put in the extra time to *dominate* the job.

No room for complacency

Week 45:

☐309. "When you start demanding and receiving more from yourself, they will start asking more about you."

You want to be relevant in the community, in your workplace, or relevant in society in general, but what are you doing to create a buzz for yourself? Just going to work will not get you the voice that you want. You have to bring something to the table, you have to work towards making your vision a reality, and then people will ask about you—and maybe even help you along the way. But as long as you stay normal, you will remain normal.

☐310. "Reach for what you think is your limit, then reach for more."

Strive for the sky and once you reach it, force your way into the galaxy. I hate when people say, "The sky is the limit!" The sky itself has no limit, so neither should you. Don't ever limit your possibilities; they are endless.

☐311. "If your journey keeps you moving forward, never look back."

You should only be focused on what's ahead of you, you can't let what's behind you trip you up. The mistakes you made in the past are no longer mistakes; they are experiences because you have learned from them. They will help mold you into the person you will soon become. You have come a long way, so don't look back because that's the wrong way.

☐312. "If nothing drives you, that means you are content with your life, complacent with your salary, satisfied with what you already have, and you don't want more."

Nobody can want anything for you as much as you can want it for yourself. *Something* has to drive you to want more, whether it's a family member, a motivational speaker, or the fact that you just want better for yourself, but you need to find something to push you to get the most out of your life. Otherwise, year after year you will be stuck in the same spot, with all that unreached potential.

☐313. "Don't allow your life to function. Design the life you have always envisioned for yourself."

You allow others to control your life to the extent of determining how much you get paid, when you can go on vacation, what time to wake up, and how much time you have to eat. This is *your* life, you have every opportunity to design it and live it how you want to. It will take a lot of work because most of us want the finer things in life, but despite the hard work, whatever you want *is* obtainable. Nothing is impossible; you just have to work extremely hard. The problem is that most of us aren't willing to do that, so we settle for others telling us what to do.

☐314. "As soon as a caterpillar feels and thinks their world is over, they blossom into a butterfly."

Life gets rough. I mean, you may get to the point where you begin to ask yourself, "What is the point of living anymore?" You start to question, "Does anyone care?" and, "Why do these things keep happening to me?" Just know that you aren't the only one going through something, and never feel that you should throw in the towel on life. Life is too precious, and too many people *do* care about you. Keep pushing through life and before you know it—just when you think you are at your breaking point—that's when you will start to see change. You must first endure some trying times to appreciate the good times, but trust me, better days are coming.

☐315. **"Keep pushing the envelope, sooner or later the world will receive your message."**

Continue to chase your dream with everything you have. Before you know it, you won't be the only one believing and supporting your vision. The key is staying disciplined at all times, sacrificing what you have now for what you want later, and treating everyone with respect. You are who you think you are.

Leave nothing in the tank

Week 46:

☐ **316. "Stop discounting yourself, know your worth. People won't value you until you value yourself."**

Value yourself like a Bentley; they never go on sale, you never see a commercial for them, and they are of rare siting. Only an elite group of people can afford the car; it's *that* high in value. Treat yourself like a Bentley; stop making yourself so accessible to people who bring no value to your life. You *are* one of a kind. You are a unicorn, very rare, so carry yourself that way.

☐ **317. "I'm here to tell you that if you are waiting on the perfect time, you might as well forget about it. There will never be a perfect time; you have to create it. The time is now."**

Perfect timing does not exist; you either have to make it happen, or you can just forget about it. When you second-guess when to do things, you allow doubt and fear to sink in. Don't do that! Make your move and make adjustments along the way. A journey of 1,000 miles begins with one step. Your time is now—well, it should have been yesterday—and you can't bank on tomorrow; you don't know if you will see it.

☐ **318. "You will never be where you want to be because you keep doing the things you *want* to do."**

To get to your dreams, there are a lot of things you *have* to do that you don't *want* to do. You've got it all wrong if you think what you are doing now will get you to your destination. The journey is about growing every day and sacrificing every day. Don't be too stubborn to sacrifice for your own good.

☐319. **Everyone thinks their plan will work until life punches them.**

You think you got the perfect plan to become successful, don't you? Well, you will continue to feel that way until you experience failure, and until you feel like everything is going wrong. Don't get down, things might have gone wrong in that moment, but get back to work! Just because life hits you in the face, or you have failed, doesn't mean it's the end of the world. Hit life back with perseverance!

☐320. **"When you pray for rain and get it, know that mud follows."**

Be careful what you ask for, you just might get it, and you won't be ready for it. When you want things, you usually want the glamour you see that comes with it. No one thinks about the hardship that comes with wanting whatever it is they want. Make sure you can handle what you ask for, both the positive and the negative sides of it. Everything that glitters isn't gold.

☐321. **"When living and working for a purpose stronger than yourself, hard work is a necessity, not an option."**

Some people work hard because they choose to, and there's nothing wrong with that, but the people who work hard— because it's the *only* option they have—are the ones you have to look out for. They have a drive and a purpose. They will conquer anything in their path; they have a different level of hunger, and a higher level of tolerance than the norm. Try to find a purpose that helps you create that mentality.

☐ **322. "You need to realize that at any point in time it could all be over, maybe then you will change."**

Today could be it for you as far as your life, your job, and your relationships go. You just never know. You need to learn to cherish things more; we take everything for granted because we have access to them on a daily basis. It isn't until you lose something that you realize just how important that thing was. Be more grateful for everything you have, for nothing is promised.

Live your purpose

Week 47:

☐323. "The good thing about your bad moments is that they're only temporary."

While the moment is only temporary, you feelings can allow you to spend too much unwanted time there. Don't dwell on the bad moments; they are just that, moments. They don't last forever, remember that. Instead, you should focus on the good that follows *after* the trying moments.

☐324. "Until you are comfortable with yourself you will continue to let what others say and think affect you."

You have to be comfortable with who you see in the mirror, and if you don't like it, then it's on you to change into the person you want to be. People will always speak on your life, but the more you accept yourself, the less weight their words have. Be happy with what you see and what you possess, and let the negativity push you to achieve more.

☐325. "You are either the hunter or the hunted. Every day you have to get moving, whether you're chasing a dream or running to the next one. There isn't time to stand still."

A hunter has to eat and the hunted wants to survive, either way they are both running. Are you running to live, or are you running to eat? Get up and get moving, or become someone else's meal. It's your choice.

☐326. **"You have come a long way, so don't look back because that's the wrong way."**

Life is all about growth. Whether you want to believe it or not, you have grown as person in many ways and in so many different areas of your life, whether it's knowledge, finances, or relationships. Don't look back because you can get caught up on what's behind you, and that will only distract you. You are not in that same old place anymore; you should be focused on moving forward and uplifting yourself to new heights on all levels, and looking back won't allow that.

☐327. **"Your life is your message to the world, make sure it's helpful and inspiring."**

We all have people who look at us and feel a certain way, whether it's inspired, disgusted, proud, or ashamed. To sum it up, your life is a book that many people will one day read. Your story is one that tells of how you treated people, how you reacted to different people, and it tells of your work ethic. You have the ability to change your message. Think as if you were someone else, how would you feel about the person you are? If you don't like how you see yourself, you probably should change.

☐328. **"Be too determined to be defeated and too positive to be doubtful."**

Many people taste failure, but only the resilient decide to continuously get up after being knocked down. You have to ask yourself, "Am I that person? And if not, "Why not?" If you are uncomfortable with defeat, you will never be successful. Even in the midst of a trying time, remaining positive mentally is a part of the battle. Your mindset in the situations you face can change the outcome, but if you are never positive or optimistic, you will always end up unhappy.

☐329. "Stop looking for what doesn't help you grow."

Just because it looks good doesn't mean it's right for you. You should be chasing greatness, anyway. If you decide to chase greatness, the things that hinder you will eliminate themselves. It all starts with a choice, and the choice starts with you. A choice of sacrifice is your first battle.

Place your bets on YOU

Week 48:

☐**330. "You don't have to limit yourself to only thinking outside of the box, have the mentality where there *is* no box."**

Whatever you think is impossible, it's not. If you understand that nothing is impossible, then don't limit yourself to a box. For example, people say, "Think outside the box." No, that's wrong! Have the mentality that there is no box; the possibilities are unimaginable to the people who don't possess an imagination.

☐**331. "You can either let tragedy destroy you or motivate you."**

Tragedy is something we all have to deal with. I'm sorry to tell you, but it can't be avoided. The tragedies we face might be death, the loss of a job, sickness, or even homelessness. The question is, will you let it pull you down or pump you up? You might have a legit reason to be down and out and to feel sorry for yourself, but ask around to see who really cares. People will give their condolences, and in less than a week, the attention will no longer be on you. Will you stay down, or will you use your tragedy as fuel? Just because you get knocked down doesn't mean you *stay* down. Get back up, and continue fighting.

☐**332. "If you didn't know, you can fail while doing things you don't want to do, so you might as well take a chance at something you love."**

Many people have jobs they don't enjoy just because those jobs are safe; they offer health benefits, they get paid vacations, and the job might not be so demanding. But what happens when you get fired? What happens when you get laid off? What happens when there are pay cuts? That's the same thing as failing. Wouldn't you rather fail at something you love? Pursue what you love. You'll never know the outcome of any situation, but don't fail at it by not even attempting. A regretful life isn't much of one.

☐333. "The things that exist today were once thought to be impossible. Those things were created by people no smarter than you."

Many of the people who created the things we use on an everyday basis aren't geniuses, and they aren't smarter than you. They just had a vision and pursued it. The problem with you is that you have a vision and you constantly talk to others, trying to get their approval. Whose approval do you really need? The key is that *you* have the vision, not someone else. Therefore, no one else will put in as much work as you should for your own dream. You don't have to be a genius for your dreams to come true.

☐334. "The tougher the battle, the sweeter the reward will be."

Stop complaining about how hard things are right now. I promise you that you are not the only one going through problems; they are simply a part of life, so deal with them. Most of your problems are things that you *can* control, but you would rather sit around and talk about them. Just know that your reward for enduring the struggle will be great. You don't go through those trials for nothing. There are blessings and lessons after every trial and tribulation.

□335. "The greatest investment to make is an investment in yourself."

Nobody should be willing to give you more than you are willing to give yourself. What you invest in yourself shows how much you value yourself and what you believe you are worth. People who do not believe that they can achieve much or that they can accomplish any of their goals will not put in the time and the money to fail. It just doesn't make sense to fuel a mission you know deep down isn't going anywhere. You are your biggest investor, put all of your eggs in one basket—*your* basket—and your return will be unimaginable.

□336. "You have to stop holding onto fears, that's keeping you from chasing your dreams."

Fear of failing is the number one thing that keeps people down. How can you continuously see what you want in life and not chase it? When you see other people enjoying their success, you tend to be jealous. Don't be mad at them or envious of them—they took the risk and they invested. You still have the chance, but it won't last forever. Make a choice. I say chase happiness.

It's about your happiness

Week 49:

☐337. "Are you living your dreams or your fears?"

The answer to this does not mean that you have achieved your dreams if you say that you are living them, but what it *does* mean is that you are pursuing them. Chasing happiness is the goal, and you are not promised to reach your dreams if you chase them. Remember, in chasing your dream, you are overcoming your fears of failure and separating yourself from mediocrity. When you live your fears, you allow them to dictate your life, from what you do, where you go, to how you act. That's putting yourself in a box, don't do that!

☐338. "Don't ever let the reason you failed be because you didn't work hard enough."

If you are going to pursue your dream, go all out! There's no point in going 70% or 80%. Give it your all and not just your best because your best leaves room for inconsistencies. With your all, the only thing left for you to do is pass out from putting in so much work.

☐339. "Become what you really want to be, even if it takes years. Don't listen to the naysayers, and overcome the obstacles."

You can accomplish anything you want to. It might take you some time, weeks, months, or years. Nobody knows. I do know this, if you quit or don't even try, you won't feel the sense of achievement, and you will never be at peace with your decision to quit. Imagine spending day after day living with regret, no one wants to feel like that. So, go after whatever it is you want, endure the battles that come with it, enjoy the journey, and celebrate the process.

☐340. "The simplest way to reach success—which is easier said than done—is having the ability to get up every time you get knocked down."

Many people will offer advice on the different ways to become successful. There's one thing you need, and that is resilience. You have to be able to take getting knocked down 99 times and be willing to get up 100 times. Dust your back off, and keep pushing for what you want. Keep your head high, and let your vision continue to guide you. It will be tough to stick with it, but it *is* worth it.

☐341. "What is it that makes *you* happy? Don't worry about what people say or think."

Your life is your own; use it to do whatever it is you want to do, and along the way inspire others to do the same. You cannot allow other people to influence you, or to determine how you live your life. Life is about love and happiness; you should do whatever gives you those feelings. Once you gain that experience, inspire others to do the same.

☐342. "Take the responsibility for your own success, regardless of the circumstances."

You have the right to be successful. You must develop the work ethic and a mentality to overcome adversity. With a competitive and resilient attitude and a drive that knows no boundaries, you are in control of your future. Don't let your current or past situations mentally dictate your future. By that I mean, don't let whatever happened in the past make you think that you aren't worth more or that you can't achieve better.

□343. "Whining and crying only works for babies; they have no other choice. You aren't a baby, so stop acting like one."

Complaining never gets anyone anywhere unless you are a baby. Babies depend on other people because they can't do anything for themselves. You aren't a baby; you can walk, talk, work, and feed yourself, but you are just too lazy. Stop crying about all of the stuff you have to do; it's life and it's time for you to grow up and act your age.

You have to sacrifice

EARL JACKSON

Week 50:

☐344. **"Are your dreams worth you waking up two hours earlier and going to sleep two hours later?"**

We all have visions, which lead us to our dreams. We might even plan how we want to reach them. But just because you have a plan doesn't mean that is the route you *must* take. Sometimes, there is a change in the plan, which requires more sacrifice than anticipated and more time than calculated. You have to be willing to sleep less and wake up earlier consistently; you must be able to put in as much time as possible towards your dream. Don't waste time sleeping!

☐345. **"If you are making excuses before you make an attempt, you have already given up. Mentally, you've thrown in the towel."**

More than half of the battle to achieving your dreams and your goals lies in actually believing that you can do it with no doubt in mind. You don't have to know how or when you will accomplish your dream, just know that you will, and you must be willing to do whatever it takes, for as long as it takes. If you don't have that mindset and you have doubt, you are going into the battle already injured.

☐346. **"Every time you make an excuse, you are displaying your weakness."**

Excuses are for the unmotivated and the weak-minded. Stop trying to justify why you can't or won't achieve your goals. Stop being a victim of your excuses; they will hold you hostage, keep you from that job you want, keep you from that degree you want, or keep you from that house or that car you want. When you stop making excuses, you show the inner strength you never knew you had, and when you tap into that potential, you can live your dream and beyond.

☐347. "Sometimes to pursue your dreams, you have to stray away from the path you once thought was the way to go."

Just because you have a vision doesn't mean you have to know how to get there. It just simply means you know *where* you want to go. It is up to you to explore every way possible to get to your dreams and your goals. Every path will be different; some will lead you the opposite way, and some will lead you in the right direction; you just won't know it at the time. It's up to you to continue to search for the path to your goals. Many people share the same goals, but none share the same exact path. Our paths may be similar, but they are not all the same. Stay true to your vision, embrace the journey, and have faith in your path, no matter how long it takes.

☐348. "Life forces us to grow; there is no reason for you to be in the same spot year after year."

Even though we fail and have setbacks, those experiences do not stop our growth. They stunt it for a second, but in the end, they reward you with an experience that you have a chance to learn from. You must be willing to grow in all aspects of your life. You might grow in some areas more than others, and that's okay. In the end, it's all about positive growth. There is no reason you should be in the same spot today that you were in last year.

☐349. "To go someplace you have never been, you have to do some stuff you never did."

You have a daily routine that you are accustomed to, and as long as you stick to that safe, comfortable routine, you will never get better. Find your purpose in life. Program your mind to start to think differently, to move differently, and to respond and talk differently. For example, you can work on yourself by reading more, acquiring a new skill, or investing more in yourself. Stop being fearful of change and don't let it paralyze you. Fear kills dreams and hope. Be courageous and confident in yourself.

☐350. "You are still on the other side of your dream because you would rather talk than work."

It's okay to discuss your dreams, but at some point in time, you have to shut up and work. All of that talking you are doing is getting you no closer to your dream; it's just setting you back and allowing you to make excuses. The execution of a plan and the achievement of your goals and your dreams are the things that are rewarded and receive praise. Having a vision gets you nothing because you have yet to do something about your dream. More work and less talk!

Be true to your goals

Week 51:

☐351. "Your expectations can't exceed your work ethic, or you will continue to be disappointed."

You can't want more than you are willing to work for. That's like hoping for a job that you never applied for; the employer doesn't even know you exist! Put in more time, more effort, network more, and explore every option to get to wherever you want to be. It takes nothing but hard work to get what you want. Stop being lazy, you see where that got you. Try pushing harder and giving more. Be willing to fail in order to succeed.

☐352. "Don't rush things that aren't meant to be rushed."

Your dreams aren't meant to be rushed; you want the feeling of achievement and fulfillment to last, so you have to be willing to endure the struggle in order to gain that feeling. When you rush things, they don't come out exactly right. What happens if you rush while cooking? Your food isn't cooked properly, or it tastes bad. Along the same lines, if you are rushing while you are driving, you can cause an accident. Be patient, but continue to work while waiting.

☐353. "If you run around with negative and unethical people, you will pick up their ways and their attitudes about life. Hang out with encouraging and empowering people, that, too, will rub off on you."

Look at where you want to go and what you want to do in life. In doing so, you will see that you have to change your patterns, your behaviors, and that all starts with who you associate with. Most people like to see others do well, but not many want to see people doing *better* than them. You have to get away from those types of people and get around the people who will elevate you and challenge you. Your future is unlimited, but if you hang around limited people, you only limit yourself. Surround yourself with those who are where you want to be.

☐354. "Visions can't be executed when doubt and excuses are present."

How can you think clearly if you always have doubts? How can you see clearly if you are always wondering, "What if?" You will never get to where you want to go if you are always doubting yourself and making excuses. Let others doubt you and tell you why you can't achieve your goal; that's not for *you* to do. You have to be your biggest supporter and believe in yourself, even when you have every reason not to.

☐355. "Do not surrender to your emotions."

Emotions can change a situation; they can alter your decisions and how you feel. But they can also hurt you; you cannot make long-term decisions on hurt feelings or mixed emotions because you may end up living in regret. While chasing your dreams and your goals, never make decisions based on your feelings and your emotions. Some days you won't want to get up and work towards your dreams, but no one cares about how you feel when you are in pursuit of your dreams and your goals. Things need to get done, and how you feel is not a legit reason for not doing something. You better make decisions off of your principles and your purpose, and not off of your feelings and your emotions.

☐356. "In the pursuit of your dream, you probably will achieve more failures than success."

There's nothing wrong with failing, as long as you are getting up and giving it another shot. Each time you fail, you are getting closer to success. In every failure, you can only gain a learning experience by going through failure. Don't be afraid to fail; embrace it, knowing you are learning, getting better, getting smarter, getting stronger, and becoming more resilient. Failures will teach you more than success ever could.

☐357. "If you think you know what you are worth, then go out and get what you are worth."

You know what you are capable of, so why aren't you where you want to be or achieving what you want to achieve? Don't be scared to fail or afraid to take the hits of life. Those are things that will happen regardless of whether or not you are pursuing your dream, or if you are just living in your comfort zone. In the pursuit of your dream, life will test you and people will test you, so don't shy away from the test! Embrace the tests because they will make your rewards that much sweeter.

Put it all together

Week 52:

☐358. **"Just because you grew up average, learned at an average rate, and worked for an average company doesn't mean you have to *remain* average."**

Everything you like is great from your favorite singer, your favorite actor, your favorite athlete, to your favorite movie, but *you* are average. Stop spending time admiring the greats while you remain average. If you admire the greats, work hard just like the greats do. It's easier to watch what the greats do, listen to what they have to say, and watch them perform in the movies, but it's hard to put the same amount of work in when it comes to your own life. Try it, you never know what situation you might put yourself in. Who knows, it could be a *great* one.

☐359. **"Self-confidence is a skill that you must possess or work towards in order to be successful."**

Self-confidence is skill, and it's only taught through countless repetitions of whatever it is you want to be good at. For instance, if you play basketball and you are a horrible free throw shooter, you might be terrified of going to line because you are not comfortable there. By practicing and shooting the right way countless times, you will develop self-confidence when it comes to going to the line. Eventually, you will start to hope the opposing team will foul you because that's where you can dominate. In anything you do, you want to be great at it. You must repeat the process over and over again until you gain the needed self-confidence, so that when the opportunity comes, you will kill it because you have been practicing and preparing for it.

☐360. "What type of nutrition are you feeding your mind?"

What do you watch on TV? What do you listen to as far as music goes? What are the topics of your discussion? What social events do you attend? Those are all questions that represent a bigger part of being successful. Everything you do should have something in common with your goals and your dreams. If not, you will always be fighting the temptation to do something harmful to your dream instead of putting in the extra work that'll help you reach your dreams and your goals.

☐361. "Build your abilities and work on growing your mindset."

You build your abilities by studying whatever it is you want to achieve, learning the ins and outs. Experiencing failure, overcoming adversity, showing resiliency, and continuously stepping up to the challenge are good ways to develop your mind. In the challenge to develop your mind, don't try to cheat your way through it. Study your failures and see how much you can learn from it. Doing so will allow you to think totally different from the average human being. Always think outside of the box, and your level of optimism will allow you to believe that the improbable is not as tough as others think.

☐362. "If you aren't, you should be in the pursuit to become something greater than what you are now. Know that where you are now is temporary; it's just a pit stop on your life-long journey."

Where you are right now is not your permanent place in life; you will get to a better place, if that's what you work towards. If you don't work towards getting to a better place, you will digress. Life is about growth; it's not about staying the same.

You have to push every day for growth, and during that push, you can distance yourself from complacency, contentment, and digression. The things you want in life are ahead of you, so move forward, not backwards. It's all about progression.

☐363. "You have to be willing to sacrifice your happiness for your dreams."

You have to develop the mentality of doing what you hate to do, while doing it like you love it. That mindset will take you farther than you ever thought you could go. If you attack your dreams like that all of the time, you will not only reach your dreams, but you will conquer them and reach heights you couldn't have imagined. Now, just because you attacked them with that mindset does not exclude you from adversity; that will always be a part of equation, but you can defeat it with your perseverance.

☐364. "We all have the same 24 hours, but the difference between successful people and the people who talk about it is the work ethic."

Work ethic can't be taught, but it can be developed. The best way to develop your work ethic is when you have something motivating you to become successful. Many people go so hard because of the loss of a loved one or for their kids' future. Also, a person can be motivated just from the fact that they are sick and tired of settling for average and mediocrity, and they just want a better lifestyle by any means necessary. Find your motivation and use your 24 hours in a goal-oriented way.

Even the last second counts

Week 52 & a half:

☐365. "You can possess the energy and the brain power of success, but the real key is developing good habits."

If you have the energy and all you need upstairs, the next step is doing it consistently. That's what separates the successful from the unsuccessful. The lazy and unmotivated people get tired of doing the same thing and not seeing the results fast enough; they possess no patience. You have to make what you hate doing look and feel like you love doing it, and you *must* make this a habit. It has to be second nature. You have to be willing to work the days, the nights, the weekends, the holidays, and the vacations when you rather be somewhere else. Develop successful work habits, and watch success as it begins to unfold in due time.

Have you reached your goals?

www.ingramcontent.com/pod-product-compliance
Lightning Source LLC
Chambersburg PA
CBHW061817040426

42447CB00012B/2689